CITTA
NADI

River of Consciousness

HOW THE WORDS OF ALBERT EINSTEIN
REVEAL THE FLOW OF SPIRITUAL KNOWLEDGE

———

MARY LORELLO GONZALEZ

Text copyright © 2019 by Mary Lorello Gonzalez
All rights reserved
Book production by Craig Lancaster

Printed in the United States of America.

Published by Lancarello Enterprises, P.O. Box 63, Boothbay, ME 04537

ISBN-13: 978-0-9976433-2-9

For Daniel, my love, with whom I strike
a perfect balance of brain and heart.

"The most beautiful thing we can
experience is the Mysterious."

—*Albert Einstein*

Contents

Foreword

"Science without religion is lame,
religion without science is blind."

—*Albert Einstein*

Albert Einstein was man who, I believe, had the ability to tap into his scientific brilliance in a spiritual way by fully accessing his mind and soul. Much of his brilliance lay in his ability to make the heart-mind connection, whether he intended to or not.

The way we acquire knowledge depends on how open we are to receiving it. *Citta Nadi* is a Sanskrit phrase that means "river of consciousness." Literally translated, *Citta* means "consciousness," or "the mind," and *Nadi* means "conduit or a channel through which the life force travels." (Feuerstein, 2007) If we close off the Nadi, or channel, we deprive ourselves of the expansion of the mind and heart that we came here to experience as humans. One way we open the pathway is by engaging in spiritual practices. I believe Einstein continually kept his pathway to knowledge clear and was able to receive information freely and fluently.

For years, I embarked on a spiritual journey, often turning to ancient texts, philosophies, and religions including, but not restricted to, Buddhism, Hinduism, Christianity, Native American, and other Indigenous cultures. I found that many of Albert Einstein's ideas about life were very much in alignment with what I was studying and experiencing. But he was a scientist and mathematician, which in my mind had nothing to do with the mystical world. It left me with some questions about a possible connection between the science he was discovering and his own spirituality. These questions prompted me to research his personal life and examine his correspondences and quotes. I wanted to know more about his curiosities, his beliefs, and the source of his brilliance. How did he open himself up to the mathematical knowledge that seemed to flow to him so effortlessly? What did he do to allow such knowledge and genius to stream into his consciousness? How did he live his life based on his beliefs? Was he happy? Was he enlightened?

As I dove into Einstein's work and personal life, I

soon discovered that he was able to separate beliefs he had about the unknown from his proven knowledge of the universe and physics. He had a personal set of ideas and practices that helped him to expand his mind and heart to the wonders and mysteries of the universe. In his adulthood, Einstein did not believe in religion. He claimed he did not believe in God in the way God was portrayed in religion, and he was not one to follow religious dogma or doctrine of any kind. He did, however, seem to think there was some force greater than humankind, which he felt most connected to while immersed in his observation of nature and the laws of the universe. He expressed this when he said, "Everyone who is seriously involved in the pursuit of science becomes convinced that a spirit is manifest in the laws of the Universe—a spirit vastly superior to that of man and one in the face of which we with our modest powers must feel humble. In this way the pursuit of science leads to a religious feeling of a special kind, which is indeed quite different from the religiosity of someone more naïve." (Pais, 1994 p. 117)

So now my question was this: Why can't science and spirituality co-exist? Why can't a spiritual awakening occur in a soul that also feeds a scientific mind? It seemed that Einstein lived his life in a practiced spiritual way, giving him the ability to tap into his brilliance and direct his focus onto science with such precision. He loved the earth and cosmos and demonstrated an impassioned interest about the interconnectedness of humans to nature and nature to the universe. His curiosity and the way he reveled in his earthly surroundings were what drove him to want to know more and understand its complexities. He made sense of the world around him mainly through mathematics. It was a concrete language that he spoke fluently and understood. But knowledge still finds its way to us whether we acquire it through the language of math or physics or through a spiritual modality. I think he had a remarkable capability to comprehend both. Paul Ghosthorse (2013), a spiritual teacher and historian of his own Lakota culture, illustrated it this way: "Scientists look for truth in nature. As followers of the Natural Way, we [also] look for truth in nature. We don't have any conflict with science. It doesn't destroy our theology when we learn more about the world. It just deepens our appreciation for how magnificent it is." I believe Einstein would have agreed!

There are volumes to be written about the relationship between science and religion. I will leave that for you to explore on your own. For now, we will put the science aside and focus on sacred ancient teachings and philosophies accentuated by the notions of Albert Einstein, a man who, I believe, was more enlightened than he or many others dared to acknowledge.

Disclaimers

- It is important that I make it understood that the

meanings of Einstein's quotes stated in this book are purely my own interpretations and are subject to each reader's individual interpretations as well. It does not necessarily mean I believe Einstein intended the stated meanings when he uttered some of his words. The quotes and ideas spoken by him and discussed here are merely used as jumping-off points to each spiritual teaching presented. Further, nowhere will I posit that the spiritual principles stated here were definite beliefs held by Einstein. That said, I firmly believe that he lived his life in a way that kept him centered, focused, and spiritually balanced, whether it was his conscious intention or not.

• Everything presented in this book is purely for the consideration and interpretation of the reader. All I ask is that you move beyond what your mind perceives as truth and expand your idea of any and all possibilities.

• I also want to state that I don't claim to be a scientist by any means and can only understand it on its surface, as it is presented in layperson's terms. Any references I make to Einstein's theories, Newton's Law, or any other scientific concepts are derived from basic knowledge and sources cited on the reference page.

• In the cited examples and anecdotes, I have tried to re-create events and conversations as best as I can remember them. I have changed the names of individuals, places, and details such as physical properties and occupations in the interest of preserving others' anonymity.

• All quotes were taken from brainyquotes.com cited

on the reference page at the end of this book. All other sources are cited throughout the book and are included on the reference page.

- One final clarification: The terminology for the concept of a higher consciousness will be used interchangeably. Words such as source, universal life force, universe, collective conscious, collective, higher self, higher power, greater intelligence, infinite intelligence, great spirit, divine, divine power, inner being, and God all stand for that vibrational energy beyond our physical bodies and from which all living things are created.

Introduction

"It is better to believe than disbelieve. In doing so, you bring everything into the realm of possibility."

—*Albert Einstein*

A s you open this book, open your mind. There are some ideas that may be new to you. Regardless of what you have been taught or what you grew up believing, there are always endless possibilities to ponder about life and our universe. What an exciting concept! Einstein wouldn't have entertained the far-reaching concepts about the universe had he not had a mind open to any and all possibilities. Isn't it more fun to wonder about the possibilities than to close your mind to them?

Life becomes real when you begin to believe in the unreal. As you turn the pages, keep this notion in mind.

In the next few chapters, we will explore life and our purpose emphasized by the ideas of a brilliant man, Albert Einstein. I believe he was attuned to his higher self and had his own unique belief system based on what he knew (and didn't know) about the physical universe. He has admitted that he had his own "religious feeling of a special kind" (Pais, et al.,1994 P. 117), meaning he didn't believe in the conventional religious teachings of his time but rather had his own belief system. Wherever his faith rested, I believe his source of knowledge was channeled from a divine collective of non-physical consciousness, and his brilliant mind was open to this source of knowledge because of the way he lived his life and his truth. Throughout the book, we will learn about this collective consciousness, as it is so prominent in our vibrational universe.

Now is the time to reach for the pursuit of spiritual alignment and achieve an awakening of the spirit by exploring and learning from Einstein's ideas about life. As you follow the lessons in the next few chapters, I hope you will be more closely aligned with your own greater intelligence, and higher self, than ever before. You will discover a new way of looking at life, understand the bigger picture, feel happier, and experience new a love of life.

L et's begin by thinking about mass and energy. Einstein talked about these concepts, often stemming from his theory of relativity. He had this to say about it:

> "It followed from special theory of relativity that mass and energy are both but different manifestations of the same thing—a somewhat unfamiliar conception for the average mind."

What we know to be our soul is made up of energy. Our physical bodies are mass. Perhaps this isn't exactly what Einstein's words were referring to, but I choose to interpret this particular quote in this way: We are one and the same, both mass and energy. However, it is difficult for us to understand the spiritual energy realm from the point of view of the physical. This is because we, as physical beings, have lived for so long in the physical realm that we have forgotten about the vibrational or energy part of us (our soul). We have difficulty comprehending anything beyond our physicality. That is why it is important to keep an open mind. That which is beyond our ability to experience with our physical senses is a very large part of us and our universe. There is so much we do not know, and just because we cannot realize it from our physical perspective does not mean it is non-existent. Even Einstein himself said "Out yonder there was this huge world, which exists independently of us human beings and which stands before us like a great eternal riddle, at least partially accessible to our inspection and thinking" (Pais et al., 1994 P115).

With that concept in mind, I want to introduce three leading principles that I believe hold the key to spiritual awakening. Once understood, these principles, described in the next few pages, will put you well on your way to a joyous and awakened existence. Then everything else will naturally fall into place. This book will take you further on that journey, but use these three principles as your guideposts.

Leading Principle #1

There is a divine energy that lies within
all living things on earth

The first leading principle refers to this divine energy in the way that suits your sensibility. A greater intelligence. A higher power. We all come from this same source. It is that vibrational part of ourselves which we call our soul, our inner spirit. It's what some might call God. The Upanishads are ancient Sanskrit texts that are the basis of such religions as Hinduism and Buddhism. In the Isa-Upanishad, it is written that "Whatsoever exists in the universe, should be covered by the Lord. We cover all things with the Lord by perceiving the divine presence everywhere. When the consciousness is firmly fixed in God, the conception of diversity naturally drops away; because the One Cosmic Existence shines through all things" (Upanishads, 2015).

To further explain this, let me take you on an adventure. Before you were born. you were vibrational in nature and were immersed in a pool of non-physical source energy. You were excited to jump into to this life on this planet so you could have an adventure living as a human being. You understood your purpose, which is to love and create and therefore expand. You chose to do so in this form, in this lifetime, on this earth. The adventure was to experience life in physical form and to have access to material objects that you can explore through your five new senses. As a vibrational being, you did not have the ability to interpret life through vision, hearing, touch, smell, or taste. But here was a chance to experience this new way of life, and you were eager to take that plunge. So a physical being was created and your vibrational spirit gave it life force energy. And then, voila! Out you came from your mother's womb to begin your journey on earth in human form.

If you've ever seen babies go through developmental stages, you've noticed that their days are spent in an ongoing task of exploring their senses. It seems like that's all they're interested in. As soon as they are able to pick up objects, they will touch everything they can get their hands on. They closely examine objects, put objects in their mouth or up to their nose, and listen intently to every new sound. You did this as you experienced life for the first time, and you thoroughly enjoyed every minute of this new way of interpreting reality. But as you grew and continued from infancy, you became used to living life physically, and you began to lose your awareness of the vibrational energy—the higher power—that continued to be a part of you and everyone else.

Many of you as adults long to get back in touch with that God-like part of you. You may not realize that is what you are longing for. It may feel like an emptiness, a void, or a wanting for something more. Some turn to religion for answers to this yearning. Some take up yoga or meditation or go on a spiritual journey to a faraway land. Most don't realize until they start to become spiritually awakened that the answers lie within themselves. The answers you are seeking come when you once again unite the physical part of you with the vibrational, greater intelligence that has been with you all along. And then you begin to remember the wholeness of that vibrational energy that lies within all things. **This is a major key to spiritual alignment**. When you find your way back to your original intention—to love, create, and expand— you will become the whole spiritual being that you came forth to be. And when you understand that this is the purpose of all living things when they chose to reside, love and create here on this earth, you understand the divine connection we have to one another woven together by the one thread we call God.

Einstein seemed to understand this idea of the alignment of spirit and oneness with all living things. He seemed to have discerned the balance and symbiotic relationship between the physical and spiritual worlds. This is evident in the way he lived his life and in the truths he spoke.

Leading Principle #2

This divine energy has great love for us, for you.

The love of the divine is greater than anything you can even imagine.

You were created out of this divine love, and you are held high in it, not one more than another. All living things on earth and in the universe have the ability to tap into this greatest love, always have access to it, and must know and remember that you are truly worthy of it. The greater source is not capable of experiencing you in any other way.

You are experienced only as pure and lovable in the eyes of your source. And as you are made up of the same divine energy that created you, you also have the ability to share this great love with others unconditionally. This includes, most importantly, yourself. The love in all of us is ever expanding, and our purpose here is to perpetuate that expansion.

Leading Principle #3

Thoughts are energy

Once our thoughts are birthed by us, they are sent forth into the universe. From that point on, they can be very powerful. All creations begin with a thought. All manifestations of physical things begin with a thought. Someone had to imagine everything that was created here on earth. Whether it is a painting, a building, a cell phone, a computer or a desire coming into fruition, we can manifest anything we want beginning with an idea. Just the same, we can attract anything we want into our lives with our thoughts. This is a universal law most commonly known as the Law of Attraction. If you focus your attention on one thing, whether it's for a second or an hour, you will that very thing into your experience. Hasn't this happened to you? You are thinking about something and suddenly you see a picture of it or someone mentions it? You may think you have had a psychic episode, but that may not necessarily be the case. This is simply the laws of the universe at work. If you continue to focus on one thought, more ideas, information, and objects having to do with that thought will come into your experience.

Remember, that vibrational part of us is made up of energy, and our thoughts are energy as well. We are physical beings. Our thoughts can turn into physical things that we can appreciate in our life in the physical realm. There will be more on this basic principle—the law of attraction—later in the book.

These three principles—that we are of great intelligence in human form, that there is a great love for us that we always have access to, and that thoughts are energy and powerful—changes your perspective already, doesn't it?

As you read on, keep these three key principles in mind. There will be nine lessons, referred to as postulates, presented here, and all are based on these leading principles and inspired by Einstein's ideas about the universe and life. If you understand and accept these three principles, then the nine lessons to follow will be simple and will help nurture your spiritual awakening.

With each lesson, you will have a week of guided reflection and practice so that you can fully understand and incorporate them into your life. Here's the weekly schedule:

Monday: Read and reflect on the postulate. Take some time to really read and understand the concept or idea being introduced. I will share my interpretation of Einstein's words. Think about how you might interpret them as well.

Tuesday: Learn and perhaps create some affirmations that you will practice daily. Affirmations help you create new habitual thinking, which brings these positive ideas into your everyday life. The late Dr. Wayne Dyer explained it best when he said, "Affirmations are a way of allowing yourself to retrain your mind, to create a habit." Keep a running list of the ones that resonate best with you. Add to the list each week so that by the end of the nine weeks you will have a comprehensive, well-rounded set of daily affirmations to practice.

Wednesday: Active practice. Try a suggested action to practice what you have learned. By executing the suggested practices, you will begin to understand how to live peacefully and aligned on a daily basis so that by the end of the nine weeks you will have adopted this lifestyle of happiness.

Thursday: Active practice.

Friday: Write about the week's journey. There will be questions guiding you to write about what you've learned and experienced in your practice of that week's lesson.

Saturday and Sunday: Meditate. Reflect on experiences using the guided meditation included in the chapter or by using your own method of relaxation and meditation.

Recordings of all the guided meditations, with music, are included with the purchase of this book. They can be accessed by going to www.harmonyspaces.net, and entering the access code CittaNadiROC. You can also scan the code at right with your phone.

Chapter One

POSTULATE #1

Read and reflect

"There are only two ways to live your life. One is as though nothing is a miracle. The other is as though everything is a miracle."

—*Albert Einstein*

An enlightened life is a happy life. It's as simple as this. You came into this world as pure love energy within a natural state of happiness. That vibrational part of yourself is pure love and joy. One sure way to get back in touch with this energy, to realign with it, is to fill yourself with love, gratitude, appreciation, and joy. This is who you really are. No one likes to go around feeling annoyed, depressed, stressed, or even merely satisfactory. It doesn't feel good. And when you don't feel good, it's your inner spirit's way of letting you know you are not in touch with who you really are. So how do you experience joy on a daily basis when there is so much going on in your everyday life? One way is to appreciate everything around you as though you are a baby looking at it for the very first time—as you did when you first came into your physical body. Life is a miracle.

Einstein had a deep curiosity about everything around him. He wanted to know and learn the processes of how things came about, how they worked, and what role humans had in this cosmic play. He was most interested in physics and understood that the perfect harmony in the music of the universe was like a symphony. There is so much that surrounds us to which we don't even give a second glance because we are stuck in our negative thoughts, busy worrying, and experiencing our world as mundane.

Lao Tzu, an ancient Chinese philosopher, wrote the *Tou Te Ching* about 2,500 years ago. In these writings he talks about four cardinal virtues to live by. The first was to have **Reverence** for all life—to practice **unconditional love** for yourself and all other beings (Tzu, 2016). It seems that Einstein understood this when he expressed his idea about living as though everything is a miracle.

There is so much to appreciate and be grateful for in our physical world. We can all appreciate a beautiful sunset, but did you ever stop to think what a miracle it is that the earth never stops turning to create those sunsets? The moon passes through its phases, each one as beautiful as the last. Snowflakes, budding flowers, a cooing baby, a train speeding along on its track. Look at them with awe and wonderment. Think about your favorite coffee that you drink every day. Appreciate with wonder what went into getting that coffee into your hands. This wonderful, thriving earth produced the coffee beans, people worked together to pick those beans, process them, transport them to the coffee shop or store, and ground them. Somebody manufactured and provided the cup. All of these people have lives. They all love somebody. They all have a story. Appreciate all it took for each and every thing you encounter to occur or manifest. There are so many things here for you each and every day that have a process or a creation either by nature or by human. The world is working in perfect harmony. A squirrel gathers its acorns while a few feet away a bird searches for worms living and working in an entirely different ecosystem all in itself. A baby's smile, an elderly couple holding hands, gas in your car, a roof over your head, a bird's song. All have a special music, a special rhythm, a vibration. The teacher who taught you to read so that you can enjoy this and any other book. Appreciate with gratitude all with which you come into contact. Have an interest, a curiosity, an enthusiasm. Feel your mood instantaneously rise to who you really are, to your higher self. When you appreciate and love life, you can match and reach a higher energy vibration—the vibration of this greater power that you are a part of and that is a part of you. When that happens, more miracles and positive manifestations will occur, and you will become closer to the divine that resides in you. And you will quickly learn that gratitude and happiness walk hand in hand.

Tuesday

Affirmations

Choose one, two, or all of these affirmations to add to your daily affirmations, and recite them every morning. Or write one of your own that affirms the miracle of everything that comes into your experience.

- Everything is a miracle.
- I notice and appreciate the harmony with which the world around me works.
- I see beauty in everything and everyone.
- I have reverence for all living things.

Wednesday

Active Practice

Now that you understand and affirm this concept of looking at life as though everything is a miracle, do it! Practice feeling appreciation for everything that comes into your experience. It can be from the smallest momentary encounter to a more prominent situation. Nothing is insignificant. This is a "stop and smell the roses" exercise. When we were vibrational beings only, before we came into human form, we perceived everything as vibration. As humans we were given senses. These senses were meant to give us a means to interpret vibration in different and interesting ways. We are now able to filter vibrations through our senses—sight, hearing, touch, smell, taste. It was new and different to us when we came into our physical bodies as babies, but it's something we have learned to take for granted as we've grown older and become more accustomed to it.

Break that cycle of ordinary experience. Go back and experience things as if you were perceiving them for the first time.

1. Eat mindfully. The next time you eat breakfast, really take the time to enjoy it. Take in the scent before you put it to your lips. When you take a bite, hold it in your mouth for a moment before chewing. Notice the variety of tastes and textures. Eat slowly and savor every bite, every sip. Really revel in how good it tastes and how it satisfies your hunger.

2. Take some time today to sit for a while and just listen. Focus on the sounds in your environment—people's voices, birds singing, leaves crunching, wind rustling, clicking of computers, laughter. Maybe even close your eyes while you are doing it. Notice different pitches, volumes, rhythms in every sound you hear. Notice which ones give you chills of pleasure and which ones make you cringe.

3. Take an object and really look at it. Take in the color and shape. Feel it with your hands and notice the texture, the temperature, the weight. Think about how it came to be. If it's manmade, ponder about how many people touched it, how it was created, how it got into your hands. If it's natural, consider the miracle of its evolution and growth and how there is not another one like it. Develop an admiration for it all.

When we revel in everyday sights, sounds, tastes, textures, and scents, they begin to become more vibrant, more significant. We begin to hold a greater appreciation for them, and for life in general. And appreciation equals happiness. It equals wholeness. It brings us closer to who we really are and reminds us of why we chose to be here.

Thursday

Active Practice

Find beauty in everyone.

This is not as easy as you think. Something humans do often is judge one another. Just as we use our senses to appreciate the beauty that surrounds us, we also use them to examine others and compare them to ourselves.

Most of the time, these judgments are unfavorable. We discount others. Or, just as damaging, we discount ourselves.

Begin this action by taking notice of how many times you judge others in a day. Note every time you have a negative opinion about someone. We tend to evaluate other people's appearance, their personality, things they say, the way they conduct themselves, their voice, their hair, the car they drive, the way they dress, their age—our judgments can be endless. Once you make yourself aware of how often you do this, you can begin to catch yourself in the act. And that's when you can turn it around and really practice the understanding that we are all created from the same higher source. We are all miracles. When you find yourself judging, immediately pause. You may even say the word "stop!" in your mind or out loud. Remind yourself that the person whom you are judging is no different from you spiritually. He comes from the same source. She has an inner being and thoughts just like you. We all love and are loved. We're mothers, fathers, sisters, brothers, aunts, uncles, children. We all feel emotions.

Now, find something to appreciate in the person you were just judging. She has good taste in clothes, he is knowledgeable about a certain subject, she has a great laugh, she is determined, he has a way with words, he is always on time for work—focus on anything positive. You may be surprised that you will always be able to find something. After you become better at this, you will find that the negative judgments will disappear and you will begin to appreciate others automatically. Your relationships will change. You will have positive expectations of others. When you see the good in others; that is how they will be present to you when you are with them. When you see them in a negative light, that's all you will see and your interactions will be negative. Remember, the law of attraction states that you get what you think about. How would you rather have it?

Here's a story that illustrates the point:

> *A woman named Kate worked with a secretary whom she perceived to be very cold. Whenever Kate interacted with the secretary, she made quiet judgments. She would think things such as "look at her clothes and hair, they're too perfect. She doesn't know how to let loose. She is always so serious." She felt uncomfortable every time she had to interact with this woman. Then, one day, Kate noticed a picture on the secretary's desk. It was a picture of the woman and her family on vacation at the beach. She was smiling, her hair was tousled, and she was embracing her children from behind. Kate began to change her perception. She realized this woman had a family she loved and nurtured. After that, every time Kate approached the secretary, she would*

first look at the picture on the desk and would hold that view of her in her thoughts as she interacted with her. Over time, she began to notice a softness about this woman that she never noticed before. She would let down her guard with Kate more, and she smiled more. Eventually they became friends and found they had a lot in common. Kate changed her expectations and attracted a softer part of the secretary's personality.

Friday

Write about your journey

1. What did you take the time to appreciate this week? How did it feel? Did you find yourself judging someone? How did you turn it around? How has your experience been with that person since you changed your expectation? Are you beginning to feel gratitude naturally without having to try? Are you appreciating life's little miracles? How does this make you feel on a daily basis?

2. Begin a gratitude journal. Every day, write 10 things you are grateful for. It could be something as simple as the bird singing outside your window or the car in your driveway. Once you have a few lists, combine them into one list and make a recording of your voice reading the items. You may even want to set it to gentle music. Then

play it for yourself as you go about your morning routine. Take note of how these two simple exercises set your mood for the day. Then watch how your life begins to improve for the better.

Saturday and Sunday

Meditation

Recordings of all the guided meditations, with music, are included with the purchase of this book. They can be accessed by going to www. harmonyspaces.net, and entering the access code CittaNadiROC. You can also scan the code at right with your phone.

Meditation Earth

This meditation will take you on a journey into space so that you can appreciate the miracle of Mother Earth from a pure, vibrational perspective. (Duration: approximately 10 minutes.)

Let's begin by finding your point of focus. It could be a steady noise in the room, a word that you repeat over and over, or your breath moving in and out.

Scan your body from feet to shoulders and neck and notice which muscles are tense. Relax and let go of the tension. Allow your body to feel open and balanced.

I'm going to guide you through a meditation ... a

journey for your mind and spirit. If your mind wanders, or if unwanted thoughts creep in, just push them gently away and turn your attention back to my voice. If you are distracted by outside noises, try your best to ignore them, and again turn your attention back to my voice.

Ready? Let's begin.

Imagine you are standing in an open field. The breeze is slightly blowing, tall grass moving ever so slightly in the distance. A feeling of peace is all around you.

You begin to feel light on your feet. You feel yourself being lifted off the ground. As you are lifted into the air, you see that you are attached to the Earth by a golden cord. Allow yourself to be lifted higher and see the grass below you. You are flying. Over the tops of trees. Over the landscape. Over the mountains. The cord is growing longer.

You are floating higher and have a view of the Earth's horizon curving into space. Rising even higher, you see the beautiful blue and white globe before you. You are filled with love for this Earth.

Now you are floating, hovering, in space, the Earth turning below.

In the distance you see small white sparks of light. They grow bigger and begin to surround you. A feeling of love and peace envelops you as this white light surrounds you. Feel the warmth and love of this light.

All is well. You are calm and peaceful as you float.

You feel the cord tugging you now. The Earth is pulling

you back. Slowly and gently you move toward Her. Back through the clouds. You sail over the landscape, over the mountains and trees, and gently back down to the ground.

The grass feels warm on your bare feet, the breeze moving over your face like a feather. There you stand by yourself. But you know you're not alone. Life is all around you.

It is time for you to return to where you were when this meditation began. As I count backward from 5, slowly feel yourself come back to this room. 4... feel your legs and feet ... 3 ... feel the ground or chair beneath you ... 2 ... slowly move your arms and hands ... 1 ... take a deep breath and open your eyes when you are ready.

Chapter Two

POSTULATE #2

Read and reflect

"I think 99 times and find nothing.
I stop thinking, swim in silence, and the
truth comes to me."

—*Albert Einstein*

I don't think you will ever find a book about spirituality and enlightenment that won't emphasize the significance of meditation. It really is key. And when you think about it, it makes perfect sense. Let's take the analogy of plumbing. When your pipes become clogged with dirt and grime, the water doesn't flow easily. You turn on the faucet and the stream is slow and trickly. Nothing works efficiently, and you become frustrated as you try harder to get the water to flow. It may even come out full of rust or soot. Your mind works the same way. When it is cluttered with negativity, worries, and obsessive thoughts, or to-do lists, thoughts that are creative, positive, and inspiring are impeded. Meditation is like pouring liquid plumbing solution through the pipes. It clears out the resistance and opens up your mind for expansion to allow inspired, even brilliant, thoughts to come forth. Einstein must have spent a good amount of time in quiet solitude to allow the brilliance of his work to emerge.

When we quiet the mind and relax the body, the magic in us is sparked. All sorts of inspired ideas and knowledge begin to come forth. If you learn how to tune in and listen, before you know it you are led in the direction of your dreams, your desires, or the knowledge you seek. Something else happens, too. You become more in tune with yourself and everything and everyone around you. Things start to fall into place. You feel better, sharper, and more alert. You worry less, laugh more, think clearly, and make sound decisions. You feel calmer and don't sweat the small stuff because you begin to understand the whole picture—the idea that you are part of a divine source that loves you so very much and will always lead you down the path to happiness. You can see that path only if you are attuned to the source energy in your higher self. And the easiest way to do that is through meditation.

Those who have changed their lives through meditation understand its power. However, if you have not experienced it yourself and you need proof, just look at the growing number of studies that confirm its success in actually changing the neuropathways in the brain. Meditation leads to clarity of thinking, less worry, better decision-making, sharper wit, more patience, and better emotional regularity. Because the intention of this book is not to provide proof of the benefits of meditation, or any other of the spiritual practices mentioned, we will not outline the studies. However, if you feel compelled to do your own research, consider looking at an article in Forbes headlined "7 Ways Meditation Can Change Your Brain." It examines studies done by institutions such as Yale, UCLA, Harvard, and Johns Hopkins that prove meditation alters your brain for the better (Walton, 2015).

So how, exactly, do we meditate? The guided meditations provided on the website are a good way to start. It's easy to tune everything else out when you are listening to the journeys that are provided for you. However, if you want to try to meditate on your own, you have all you need: your breath. In the coming pages you will find a simple guideline on how to meditate using the gift you have been given at birth—your breath.

Tuesday

Affirmations

Choose one, two, or all of these affirmations to add to your daily affirmations and recite them every morning.

Or write one of your own that affirms that quieting your mind will help you feel clear and at ease.

- My mind and body are in perfect balance.
- All that I seek I can find within.
- My spirit knows that all is well.
- I am in harmony with the universe.

Wednesday and Thursday

Active practice

Carve out at least 10 minutes each day to meditate. Try to make this part of your daily routine from here on. Countless studies have shown that just 10 minutes per day will improve your life tremendously in terms of enjoying a calmer, more peaceful existence.

There is evidence that physical health improves and that people have more clarity, less anxiety, and more self-confidence.

How to meditate

Find a quiet space and get into a comfortable position. You could sit in a comfortable chair with your legs uncrossed. Some people prefer to sit pretzel style or in the yoga lotus position.

Whatever is most comfortable for you and where the energy can flow easily throughout your body is fine.

It is your choice to play just the music or use the guided meditations from the website that go with this book. Or you might decide to sit in complete silence.

Choose something to focus on. It could be your breath going in and out, a word such as *peace* or *calm*, a chant such as "om," or a steady sound in your environment such as an air conditioner or the wind.

Turn your attention to your source of focus. If your mind wanders (which it will, many times!), turn your attention back to your breath or whatever you have chosen as your point of focus.

Relax your body, sink into the Earth, and allow the love to flow through you. Do this for about 10 minutes daily.

Friday

Write about your journey.

How are you feeling in general? Are you beginning to think more clearly? Are ideas flowing to you? Are you finding it easier to make decisions? Are you handing life with a little more ease? Do things just seem to fall into place lately? Are you feeling calmer? More alert?

If just a couple of days of meditation have improved your general well-being, imagine what a regular routine will do!

Saturday and Sunday

Chakra meditation

Recordings of all the guided meditations, with music, are included with the purchase of this book. They can be accessed by going to www.harmonyspaces.net, and entering the access code CittaNadiROC. You can also scan the code at right with your phone.

This Chakra meditation is a simple meditation that you can use as part of your daily routine. (Duration: approximately 15 minutes.) The chakras are energy points that correspond with different areas of your physical body and its functions as well as your emotions. The chakras are associated with the basic colors on the rainbow spectrum.

Here is a brief description of the seven main chakras and their locations on the body:

Root Chakra: This chakra's energy center is located at the base of your spine and below. It is associated with the color red. Because it is closest to the Earth, its vibration centers on your ability to stay grounded in your physicality and basic needs. It also governs bodily functions having to do with your lower digestion tract, groin, legs, and feet.

Sacral Chakra: The sacral chakra's energy center

is located just below your naval. It is associated with the color orange. Its vibration centers on emotion, creativity, and sexuality. It also governs bodily functions having to do with reproduction, kidneys, and bladder.

Solar Plexus Chakra: The solar plexus energy center is located just above your naval. It is associated with the color yellow. Its vibration centers on self-esteem, personal power, joy, and ambition. It also governs bodily functions having to do with your upper digestion tract, muscles, and pancreas.

Heart Chakra: The heart chakra's energy center is located within your heart. It is associated with the color green or pink. Its vibration centers on love, peace, and harmony with your true self. It also governs bodily functions having to do with your heart, lungs, hands, and arms. It is where some believe the soul resides.

Throat Chakra: The throat chakra's energy center is located in the throat area. It is associated with the color sky blue. Its vibration centers on communication and speaking your truth. It also governs bodily functions having to do with your neck, shoulders, and thyroid.

Third Eye Chakra: This chakra's energy center is located on your forehead just above your eyes and is associated with the color indigo. Its vibration centers on intuition, inner vision, and wisdom.

Crown Chakra: The crown chakra's energy center is located at the top of your head and is associated with the color violet or white. Its vibration centers on your connection to the higher source. It governs bodily functions having to do with brain, nervous system, and pituitary gland.

Meditation to Open the Chakras

Let's begin by finding your point of focus. It could be a steady noise in the room, a word that you repeat over and over, or your breath moving in and out.

Scan your body from feet to shoulders and neck and notice which muscles are tense. Relax and let go of the tension. Allow your body to feel open and balanced.

I'm going to guide you through a meditation ... a journey for your mind and spirit. If your mind wanders, or if unwanted thoughts creep in, just push them gently away and turn your attention back to my voice. If you are distracted by outside noises, try your best to ignore them, and again turn your attention back to my voice.

Ready? Let's begin.

Begin by focusing your thought on your root. This is at the base of your spine. Imagine a ball of red light there. Beautiful earthy red color like the red you might see in a sunset or Arizona desert. Now imagine this red ball is spinning. As it spins, the red light is pulsing and cleansing the area. You feel grounded. You feel safe and secure and deeply rooted into the Earth. This is your basic real self. Think to yourself, "I am perfect just the way I am." Breathe into that space. Take a deep breath all the way down to your root. Hold it there. Now let it out. Feel the flowing energy of your root chakra.

Now move your attention to your sacral chakra. This is located just below the naval. Imagine a bright orange spinning ball of light. With each breath you take imagine the orange light expanding and getting brighter. You are opening your sacral energy center. Think to yourself, "Creativity is flowing. I feel free in my body." Allow your emotions to flow freely... pleasure, hope, love. Breathe into that space. Allow your breath to move all the way down to that orange spinning light. Hold it. Now let the breath out. Feel the flowing energy of your sacral chakra spinning and nourishing that area.

Now move your energy to the area of your belly. This is your solar plexus. There spins a bright, shiny, yellow ball of light. Invite that sunshiny yellow color to expand with each breath and cleanse the area. You are feeling more centered, self-confident, and powerful. Think to yourself, "I can do anything I set my mind to." Breathe into that space. Hold it there. Now let it out. Feel the flowing energy of your solar plexus energizing your power center.

Now move on up to your heart. Concentrate on the emerald green spinning ball of light. Think about a person or pet that you love unconditionally. Feel the healing green light open your heart center and expand outward. Allow the love to pour out of you. With each *breath, the light expands and nourishes your heart and spirit. Think to yourself "I am worthy of love." I give and receive love unconditionally." Breathe into that space. Hold it there. And let it out. Feel the energy of your heart chakra flowing freely.*

Move your attention now to your throat chakra located in your neck, or throat. Here the spinning ball is a beautiful blue like the color of the sky. With every breath you take, imagine the ball of light energy getting brighter and expansive. Think to yourself "I am allowed to speak my truth. The words flow freely. My words and ideas are valued." Breathe into that space. Hold it. And let it out. Feel the energy of your throat chakra flowing effortlessly.

Focus your thoughts now on your third eye located on your forehead. Picture a deep indigo light spinning and expanding with each breath you take. Think to yourself, "I am full of wisdom. My inner voice tells me exactly what I need to know." Breathe into that space of your third eye. Hold it. Let it out. Feel the energy flowing freely there.

Move up to the crown chakra located on the top of your head. A bright violet-white ball of light is spinning here. It is all-knowing and healing. It expands with every breath. Think to yourself, "I am connected to my highest self and the Universe. I understand the bigger picture beyond that which is here on Earth. I am empowered by this thought." Direct your breath up into this space. Hold it. And let it out. Feel the energy of your crown chakra flowing freely.

Now all your chakras are open. You are balanced and healthy. Travel through them one more time: red root, orange sacral, yellow solar plexus, green heart, blue throat, indigo third eye, and violet white crown. You are open and aligned.

It is time for you to return to where you were when this meditation began. As I count backward from 5, slowly feel yourself come back to this room. 4... feel your legs and feet ... 3 ... feel the ground or chair beneath you ... 2 ... slowly move your arms and hands ... 1... take a deep breath and open your eyes when you are ready.

Chapter Three

POSTULATE #3

Read and reflect

"Look deep into nature and you will understand everything better."

—*Albert Einstein*

Most physicists, Einstein included, are fascinated with the way the world around us works. Einstein had a particular reverence for the natural world and said this about it: "What I see in Nature is a magnificent structure that we can comprehend only very imperfectly, and that must fill a thinking person with a feeling of 'humility'" (Dukas & Hoffman, 1981 P. 39). I have wondered how one can study the outer workings of the universe without first looking right here in our backyard. Nature exists and co-exists in perfect harmony. It is the perfect university to help us study the laws of the universe on a smaller, more intimate scale. We can learn a lot from turning our attention to the plants and animals of this planet. As we observe them, we discover that they live and die without being caught up in the process. They take only what they need, they don't waste or destroy for the purpose of destroying. They have keen senses and agile physical bodies. They care for one another and fight their enemies only for the purpose of their own survival.

Our bodies and spirit are made up of the same elements, minerals, and molecules as this beautiful planet we call home. We are a part of her and she is a part of us. This living, breathing life force provides us with everything we need to live a full, balanced, healthy, and joyful life. She is our ultimate healer. There's something to be said about being close to other living things that keep us closer to our higher selves. We know that all living things are created from the same source. But somehow when we are with other humans, judgement and competition block our ability to be the loving beings that we came here to be. When we are among the non-human living beings of our planet, we are better able to experience a love that is unconditional, one that is without resistance. We feel intimate and connected to nature, which opens a smooth path to our higher selves and the pure love energy that flows through and around us.

Our earth is a beautiful planet with incredible

structures. It is soothing to the eye and equally pleasing to the other senses. The more devoted we are to Her, a more calm and centered feeling we hold. Think about the times you have sat on a beach or in the woods and just felt a sense of peace and tranquility. Did you ever stop for a moment to watch the birds at your feeder or a deer grazing the land gracefully? How did you feel in that moment? If you ever have the experience of swimming with the dolphins, or whale watching, you will understand a true closeness with that which is divine!

Don't forget to include the geological world as part of your experience. Just sitting on a warm rock or the silky sand of an ocean beach can instantly connect you with a higher source. Our earth is home to an abundance of gems and minerals. Some minerals make up what we know as crystals. Many believe crystals have healing properties due to their ability to vibrate and generate heat and electricity. They are also believed to channel energy that can be focused to specific mental, physical, or spiritual healing. Holding a crystal while indoors can give you a sense of connection with the natural world.

Nature teaches us. I have learned a great deal from observing the natural world. Last summer, when I was on one of my daily early-morning walks, I spotted a fox in the road. I immediately thought of my son, who loves foxes. He always encounters them and looks at them as his kindred spirit or spirit animal. It's interesting that I came upon this fox because I had been thinking about my son. I was worried about him. He had been faced with a dilemma having to do with someone from his past coming back into his life. He really didn't talk to me about it, so I was wondering how he was dealing with it and if he was OK. I tried not to put too much emphasis on thinking about it because I knew that whatever I put my attention to had the potential to manifest. I didn't want this to become a bigger problem. It was only in the beginning stages, and I wanted it to remain there. Nevertheless, no matter how much I tried to ignore it, it was on my mind. So here this beautiful fox appeared. As it walked across the road heading toward the other side, it stopped in the middle, turned its head toward me and watched as I approached. What it didn't realize (or chose not to realize) was that a woman and her dog were approaching from behind. If it had turned its head the other way, it would have seen them. But it stood there with a fearless, gentle gaze directed at me. After a moment, it trotted off into the woods. And on it went. What intrigued me was that it didn't seem concerned about me, who was directly approaching, nor was it aware of or cared about who was behind. It just stayed in the moment and went about its task. My son is like the fox, I thought. He didn't seem to be letting his past upset him. In fact, he seemed to be ignoring it, like the fox did. After all, it was behind him. He wasn't looking toward the future with anxiety. He chose to happily go about his days. When I realized this, I let go of the resistance and dropped the worry. Why should I focus on this situation and thus magnify it? My son was fine. Of course, my inner intelligence already knew that. The fox just reminded me to look there. As it turns out, the situation blew over in a matter of weeks. Lesson learned. Thank you, fox!

Do I believe that fox came into my world by chance? Absolutely not! I was thinking about my son, who connects with foxes, and he appeared. There are teachers everywhere. We attract them when we need them. We just have to tune in and pay attention to their visitations and messages.

Tuesday

Affirmations

Choose any or all of the following to add to your daily affirmations and recite them every morning. Or write one of your own that affirms that nature brings you closer to your higher self.

This week, I am introducing a quote from Chief Joseph for a wonderful affirmation:

- "The Earth and myself are of one mind."–Chief Joseph, Nez Perce
- Nature is my sanctuary.
- I look to nature for answers.

Wednesday

Active Practice

Make plans to go to someplace where you can be close to nature. You can plan some day trips or a vacation surrounding nature.

Here are some suggestions:

A nature preserve, a butterfly garden, a hummingbird sanctuary, a botanical garden, a bird sanctuary, an ocean beach, a working farm, a wooded trail, a mountain trail, a rain forest, a national park, a natural cave, the Grand Canyon, a lake or river, your own backyard! If you can, find a quiet spot. Sit or stand up leaning against a tree if you can. Allow your bare feet to touch the ground. Feel at one with the Earth.

Notice all the living things around you. Think about how you are connected to all of them, how you are all one, how you all come from the same source. As you breathe in the fresh air, appreciate the abundance of it. It is always here for you, for all things that are living on Earth. Observe animals, insects, and bugs moving about their daily lives. Take note of how you are feeling as you co-exist with everything around you. Listen to the sounds of nature. The breeze through the trees, birds chirping, the movement of water perhaps, or small animals scuffling through the leaves on the ground. What scents do you notice? Turn your gaze toward the sky. There's a whole other world out there. Imagine the infinite expansion behind the clouds as they float by. Appreciate the magnificent sun for its brilliant light and warmth. Even if it is behind the clouds, it is always there, taking care of you. Feel the cool temperature, the warm breeze, the refreshing rain, the hot sun. Whatever the weather, allow it to embrace you.

Thursday

Active Practice

Find a place where there are a lot of rocks or pebbles, like a beach, the woods, or your own backyard. See which rocks you are naturally drawn to and pick them up one at a time. The Lakota Indians and other native tribes believe that if you stay quiet and become aware, you will feel them calling to you. Take them into your hands and try to feel their energy. Listen to their message. What are they telling you?

If you have a local metaphysical store near you or a gem show in your area, go and explore crystals. See which ones call to you there. Learn and discover the healing property of each crystal and its association with physical or mental health, emotional well-being and spiritual alignment.

If something is ailing you, you might be comforted by a crystal's healing energy.

Friday

Write About Your Journey

Reflect and write about your experience of communing with nature. How did you feel before and after? Did you notice anything significant? Any small miracles? Did you encounter anything extraordinary? Write about your experience with rocks, gems or crystals. Did they call to you? Did you feel the power of their healing energies?

Saturday and Sunday

Meditation

Recordings of all the guided meditations, with music, are included with the purchase of this book. They can be accessed by going to www. harmonyspaces.net, and entering the access code CittaNadiROC. You can also scan the code at right with your phone.

(Duration: approximately 15 minutes.)

Into the Crystal Cave

Let's begin by finding your point of focus. It could be a steady noise in the room, a word that you repeat over and over, or your breath moving in and out.

Scan your body from feet to shoulders and neck and notice which muscles are tense. Relax and let go of the tension. Allow your body to feel open and balanced.

I'm going to guide you through a meditation ... a journey for your mind and spirit. If your mind wanders, or if unwanted thoughts creep in, just push them gently away and turn your attention back to my voice. If you are distracted by outside noises, try your best to ignore them, and again turn your attention back to my voice.

Ready? Let's begin.

This journey begins at the entrance of a cave. Picture yourself standing here with the bright sun bearing down on you. Its hot rays infuse you with healing energy. Now begin to move into the cave. Instantly, cool, damp air surrounds you. A salty, earthy smell fills your senses, giving you a feeling of calm curiosity. As you move farther into the cave, torches of dancing fire light your path. Continue through, running your fingers along the cool, damp, rocky walls. At the end of this tunnel, you stand at an arched opening. A vast, round, open space is before you with magnificent stalactites. Step out onto the marble floor. In the center is a pedestal made up of three large rocks. On top, a smooth, pink, rose quartz crystal. Place your hands on the crystal and close your eyes. A warm feeling of intense love begins to fill you, starting at your hands and traveling up your arms and shoulders and into your heart.

Now move into one of the other three entryways. You'll see a light glowing from the entrance, beckoning you to continue toward it. Go to it now. Enter deeper into the cave. You are filled with wonder and excitement. Continue through. Do you see the ancient symbols and pictographs? Do you feel as though you have been here before? A faint sound permeates the walls. A steady tone resonates throughout the cave. As you come to the end of the tunnel, everywhere you look are brilliant, shimmering, radiant crystals. Clear pure quartz mixed in with vibrant emerald green. All reflecting off one another, producing a magnificent, shimmering light show. In the center of the room is a circle of crystals. Sit down there. Breathe in the energy of the crystal surroundings. Feel their healing force penetrate your body. Your spirit is soaring, vibrating with the energy these crystals put forth.

Now you see the wall opening up, forming another entryway. More crystals line the walls as you make your way through. The cool dampness of the cave turns into a warm, fiery bath of what feels like sunlight. You hear the roar of fire. Deeper and deeper you walk, feeling the intense warmth of the orange glow ahead. Now you face another vast space. There is no ceiling, no floor, no walls. Just an inner sphere. At the center of this enormous spherical space is a floating ball of fire and light.

You are at the heart of the Earth. Her spirit center. The

light reaches out to you, and you feel what she is feeling. There is excitement that you are there. There is immense love for you. You communicate a loving exchange of joy and excitement. From your heart to hers.

(Pause for about a minute.)

See the rose quartz crystal in your mind's eye. It's time to go back to it. As you back away, you are filled with gratitude. Turn back up the crystal hallway into the crystal room. In the center circle is a gift for you. An emerald green stone. Take it with you as you continue back through the cave.

Now you are into the sunlight, where once again you feel its healing energy. Your feet are planted firmly on the ground. And you now have the knowledge that whenever you want, you can return here to the crystal cave and be one with the heart center of the Earth.

It is time for you to return to where you were when this meditation began. As I count backward from 5, slowly feel yourself come back to this room. 4 ... feel your legs and feet ... 3 ... feel the ground or chair beneath you ... 2... slowly move your arms and hands... 1... take a deep breath and open your eyes when you are ready.

Chapter Four

POSTULATE #4

Read and reflect

"In the middle of difficulty
lies opportunity."

—*Albert Einstein*

onflict is a catalyst for clarity. This is a difficult concept to accept. Before we can gain control over our struggles, we must understand the idea that we need discord to help us to discern what we want in life. When we realize what we don't want or like, it gives birth to what we desire. If you are unhappy with something or someone, it opens up an opportunity to decide how you want it to be different or better. For example, if you don't like things about a relationship you're in, you can then define what you do want in a mate or a friend. It all starts with a thought. Remember, thoughts are energy, and they can be powerful. If you acknowledge the struggle and begin to think about how you want something to be different, even if right now you don't think the circumstances can change, that is the first and most important step in shifting the energy and making it happen. If you keep thinking about and focusing on what's wrong, you will only attract more of what's wrong. That's the law of attraction at play. That's the power of thought. If you don't like discord, keep sending out visions about peace and harmony. If you are struggling with someone or something, keep a positive attitude. Through the contrast comes clarity. And with clarity come solutions.

There's an old adage about a butterfly struggling to get out of its cocoon. A man comes by and in an effort to help, opens the cocoon and helps the butterfly out. But instead of flourishing, the butterfly falls to the ground and dies. The struggle was necessary for the butterfly to live.

And so it is with humans.

Have you ever looked back on a difficult experience and felt grateful for it? Maybe it's because you had the opportunity to grow or gain strength. Or maybe you are proud of the way you handled yourself. Perhaps you became closer to someone or yourself during that difficult time. Or perhaps you gained a better understanding of something or someone else's circumstances. We should always be thankful for difficult experiences. They provide us with an opportunity to grow, learn, and expand.

Learn to appreciate the struggles in your life. Recognize them as opportunities. Don't forget, you have come here to experience life as a physical human being, and conflict is all part of the Earth experience. Remember, too, that your inner being knows that everything will work out for you. This is a very powerful concept. Because if you believe and trust that idea during the difficult times, you will be pleasantly surprised at how easily you will be able to come up with solutions, how your timing will be right, and how helpers, what we might even call Earth Angels, will appear seemingly out of nowhere to help carry you through.

When my son, Daniel, fell ill with an attack of appendicitis, my husband was on a 23-hour flight to China and there was no way to get in touch with him. I had to handle the situation myself, as a parent. I have never considered myself very good at making emergency room visits. That was always my husband's department. But I knew it was up to me to help my son. I decided I had to be strong and positive that it was all going to be OK.

It was fascinating how it all played out. Daniel was taken in and examined right away, and as he was being wheeled through the corridor, we ran into the father of an acquaintance of his. It turned out he was one of the hospital administrators. He saw to it that my son got into surgery immediately. Not only that, but he called in the best surgeon. Everything went smoothly. Daniel ended up getting his own room with a view of the helicopter landing pad, which he was excited about. I was able to stay with him overnight as he recovered. I wanted to be right there by his side. He and I look back with warm feelings as we are both so thankful for the time we spent together, just the two of us. It really was special. That difficult time gave me an opportunity to (a) see that I could indeed handle situations like that myself, (b) use it as an opportunity to practice keeping my mind open, creating good timing and circumstances and the perfect outcome, and (c) make the best of a difficult situation and be able to look back with good feelings.

Tuesday

Affirmations

Choose any or all of these affirmations to add to your daily affirmations and recite them each morning. Or write one of your own affirming that from conflict comes clarity.

- Things are always working out for me.
- I can stay positive and be in touch with my inner being even in the most trying situations.
- I am thankful this conflict is bringing me clarity.
- I am grateful for this struggle so I can discern the good I want to come out of it.

- In this difficult situation, I look for an opportunity for good.
- I recognize the gifts in this struggle.
- I am more than my troubles. (Wayne Dyer)
- In the midst of these troubles I still have hope.
- This too shall pass. (An oldie but goodie!)
- I will not allow anything to keep me from pursuing my dreams.

Wednesday

Active Practice

If you are experiencing a struggle, ask your inner being and source to help you to sort it out. Try to stay positive and in an appreciative mode and watch how solutions and inspirations will pop into your head or show up in other ways. For example, you might overhear a conversation about how someone else handled a similar situation, or come across a magazine article about it. Notice how the right people will be there at the right time to help or guide you. Just the act of staying positive and trusting your higher self can cause circumstances to change. If there is a person giving you a hard time and you change your thoughts about that person, your relationship could change in a positive way. Remember the story about Kate and the secretary? Maybe even something you never even thought of will occur and shift everything for the better.

A friend and I run a children's meditation group. Frequently, the kids will share stories about others with whom they are struggling. Some of them are even being bullied. We began to talk about changing their perspective and trying to see the good in others, no matter how small. We talked about the power of love and kindness. At the end of each session, we started practicing what's called a metta meditation. It's a way of sending out love and kindness to others. Try doing a metta meditation.

It goes something like this:

Begin by composing three positive phrases. Direct them to yourself.

- May I be happy.
- May I be healthy and strong.
- May I be calm and relaxed.

Next, think about someone you love and say the same three phrases with that person (or people—it needn't be one) in mind:

- May you be happy.
- May you be healthy and strong.

• May you be calm and relaxed.

Now think about someone you don't know very well. It can be anyone. The postman, a person you might see walking in your neighborhood, a co-worker. Direct the same three phrases to that person.

Then direct the three phrases to someone with whom you are in conflict. This may be difficult at first, but remember: if you send love and kindness to them, you will attract the same from them. Next, direct the phrases to everyone in the room, even if it's only yourself, and last, to everyone in the universe. This was a very powerful exercise for our students. We continually hear many stories about how their difficult relationships changed for the better. In one instance, a student eventually became friends with the person who was bullying her!

Sending out love and kindness, changing your thoughts about a situation, understanding and appreciating that conflict can give birth to new desires, asking your higher self or source for help, or simply surrendering to your source or God altogether can make a huge difference in the way difficult situations play out.

You will notice something good will always arise from the struggle, and you may even find yourself grateful for having it.

Look for the opportunities in the adversities. You will always find them.

Thursday

Active Practice

Make a Hope Box

Find a small box. Most craft stores sell small wooden boxes, or you can recycle a jewelry box or metal container that holds mints. It should be large enough to hold a few strips of paper. Decorate it with paint, fabric, stickers, stamps, any way you would like. You can even line the inside with a soft fabric, like velvet or felt.

In this box, you will place all your wishes, desires, and prayers. Anything you want to manifest can go in here. The idea is to think about the desire and then let it go. Write down your hope, wish, desire, or prayer on a strip of paper and fold it up, and then place it in your Hope Box. It's as simple as that. Now you can give it up to God and the universe. By giving it up to the universe, you are demonstrating that you trust that all will be well. And it will.

Friday

Write About Your Journey

First, write about any struggles you had this week where you were able to discover and be grateful for the lesson and/or opportunity, or where you gained clarity about what you desire. Talk about the favorable outcome.

Next, write about a time when you handled a situation with clarity and everything seemed to fall into place. Knowing what you know now, why do you think it happened that way?

Saturday and Sunday

Meditation

Recordings of all the guided meditations, with music, are included with the purchase of this book. They can be accessed by going to www. harmonyspaces.net, and entering the access code CittaNadiROC. You can also scan the code at right with your phone.

This affirmation meditation is a relaxing way to practice your affirmations and assimilate them. (Duration: approximately 5 minutes.)

Let's begin by finding your point of focus. It could be a steady noise in the room, a word that you repeat over and over, or your breath moving in and out.

Scan your body from feet to shoulders and neck and notice which muscles are tense. Relax and let go of the tension. Allow your body to feel open and balanced.

I'm going to guide you through a meditation ... a journey for your mind and spirit. If your mind wanders, or if unwanted thoughts creep in, just push them gently away and turn your attention back to my voice. If you are distracted by outside noises, try your best to ignore them, and again turn your attention back to my voice.

Ready? Let's begin.

Things are always working out for me.

I can stay positive and be in touch with my inner self even in the most trying situations.

I am thankful this conflict is bringing me clarity.

I am grateful for this struggle so I can discern the good I want to come out of it.

Things are always working out for me.

In this difficult situation, I look for an opportunity for good.

I recognize the gifts in this struggle.

I am more than my troubles.

Things are always working out for me.

In the midst of these troubles, I still have hope.

This, too, shall pass.

This struggle is necessary in order for me to grow.

Things are always working out for me.

I will not allow anything to keep me from pursuing my dreams.

Because of this conflict, I can dream more dreams.

I am hopeful, and I know that there is always hope.

Things are always working out for me.

It is time for you to return to where you were when this meditation began. As I count backward from 5, slowly feel yourself come back to this room. 4 ... feel your legs and feet ... 3 ... feel the ground or chair beneath you ... 2 ... slowly move your arms and hands ... 1 ... take a deep breath and open your eyes when you are ready.

Chapter Five

POSTULATES
#5 and 5A

Read and reflect

"The imagination is powerful.
Imagination is more important than
knowledge. Knowledge is limited.
Imagination encircles the world."

—*Albert Einstein*

I am putting these two postulates together because both
are relevant to the Universal Law of Attraction.

Postulate #5

Remember in the third leading principle we talked about how thoughts are energy leading to creation? This is a universal law known as the Law of Attraction. It states that whatever you think about or focus on will come into your experience. All that has been created began with a thought. Much of what you experience begins with imagination.

A few summers ago, I learned about a place where there was a hummingbird sanctuary. I very much wanted to visit this place. and I researched it online and made plans to visit with friends. It was very much on my mind, and I was joyfully looking forward to visiting. That summer I saw many hummingbirds, not only at the sanctuary but also in my own backyard, in the backyards of others and even in my father's tiny garden in Vermont. Because I had hummingbirds on my mind, and I was feeling positive and optimistic about them, they showed up many times in my experience that summer. I had not seen any hummingbirds before that and have seen few after that time to this date. It was my thoughts along with my desires that created that experience.

Have you ever wished for something and daydreamed about it only to realize your wish was fulfilled not long after? When I found the house I am currently living in, I knew I really wanted it, but we had to wait for the sale of our previous house to go through. So I would spend minutes a day looking at the pictures of it online and imagining myself in it. I would leave work and drive straight there as if I were coming home. And then after we moved in, my husband and I drew plans of how we wanted it renovated. We kept drawing them over and over and picturing it as we walked throughout the house. Our vision became a reality, and it all began as a thought. I once heard a story from a friend who used to drive his old minivan to work all the while imagining he was sitting in his dream car. He even went so far as taping a picture of the logo onto his steering wheel. It wasn't long after that that the car was sitting in his driveway.

Muhammad Ali once quoted Jesse Jackson: "If my mind can conceive it, and my heart can believe it, then I can achieve it" (USA Today, 2016). Imagination can take you anywhere you want to go. It can help you dream anything you want to dream. It opens up a world of infinite possibilities! When we desire something and we hold our thoughts and focus on it with appreciation and the belief that we can have it, there's no stopping us and the laws of the universe from bringing it to fruition. That dream job, relationship, career, even state of being can manifest just from your very thought of how you want it to be.

The key to tapping into the Law of Attraction is to stay in a place of gratitude and appreciation. If you focus on the positive, you will feel good and attract more positive. If you focus on negative, you can bet that you will attract more negativity and will not be happy. Einstein understood this when addressing some children at Christmastime. He wrote: "It gives me great pleasure to picture you children joined together in joyful festivities in the radiance of Christmas lights. Think also of the teachings of him whose birth you celebrate by these festivities. Those teachings are so simple—and yet in almost 2000 years they have failed to prevail among men. Learn to be happy through the happiness and joy of your fellows, and not through the dreary conflict of man against man. If you can find room within yourselves for this natural feeling, your every burden in life will be light, or at least bearable, and you will find your way in patience and without fear, and will spread joy everywhere" (Dukas &Hoffman et al., 1981 P.33) .

He was right on the mark when he said that happiness is a natural feeling. We were born in this state, and it is our natural tendency to want to remain there. The good news is that we are absolutely capable of maintaining that good feeling if we don't allow negativity to cloud our thoughts. Interesting that Einstein referenced the teachings of Jesus. He recognized that this is the fundamental message that Jesus was trying to spread.

Now consider this:

Postulate #5A

"The only reason for time is so that everything doesn't happen at once."

—Albert Einstein

I love this quote, because it's so true. Knowing now that your thoughts can manifest into reality, can you imagine if every thought you ever had culminated all at once? You would be overwhelmed! Plus, there wouldn't be any waiting time. And there is something sweet about waiting time when you are anticipating something wonderful. There is a reason for time.

Remember when you were a kid at Christmastime? Remember anticipating the day and the magic of it all? Can you recall the feeling of waiting for your birthday to come? Or your wedding day? A woman who cradles a child in her womb has quiet moments of pure joy and magic as she dreams of life with her new baby. The feeling of expectancy, coupled with the high hopes of getting what you asked for, is enchanting. The excitement of looking forward to something wonderful, intoxicating. Just the act of thinking about anything good we are anticipating gives us tingles of delight. As the time draws closer to receiving what we have been dreaming about, the excitement grows. It's a wonderful feeling. We wouldn't have words like *anticipation, looking forward to, expecting, awaiting*, or even *longing* if it weren't for the concept of time. If everything we wanted appeared the minute we thought about it, we wouldn't be able to experience the delight in waiting for it. We experience the most bliss when we are in a place where we can enjoy each moment of now while looking forward to all the gifts that are to come. If you can maintain that state, happiness and the joyful continuation of the manifestation of dreams will be forever yours.

Have you ever heard the phrases "it's all in the timing" or "all in good time" or "timing is everything"? When things are going according to plan, the plan of your higher power, you will notice that the timing will be perfect.

You will meet the right person at the right time. You will acquire the appropriate knowledge, receive a phone call or email, have a conversation, read something, have a question answered, or overhear a conversation at precisely the right time. You will hear the phrase "perfect timing!" a lot. Synchronicities will begin to occur in every aspect of your life. At first, you might think they are coincidences, but you will soon realize that divine timing is at hand.

Years ago, I was thinking about taking a beginners' class on angel card reading. I was walking along the streets of a small town near me and noticed a little shop with crystal in the window. Something made me go in there. I introduced myself to Jayda, the woman who owned the store, and she introduced me to another customer who was there with her daughter. Jayda let us know that she was very good at guessing birthdays and wanted to give mine a try. Her guess was very close, and when I revealed what it was, I was surprised to find out the other customer's daughter had the same birthday. But that wasn't all. The girl was studying to be a speech/language pathologist, which was my main profession. And if that wasn't enough of a parallel, her mom was there because she was looking for someone to do an energy clearing in her house, which was my other profession. If that all didn't line up perfectly enough, I noticed that Jayda offered classes in her store, so I inquired about one on card reading. She handed me a flyer that was sitting right on her checkout counter and said, "As a matter of fact we are offering one tomorrow night!" I couldn't have timed that visit any more perfectly.

We call these situations synchronicities. You may have heard them referred to as "God winks." When you tune in to your higher self, you will notice these kinds of things happening almost daily! It is so much fun to experience. And even more fun when you can share them with a friend who understands how this divine universe works. Almost every day, my friends and I exchange stories about divine timing. Here is one of my personal favorites:

Being that the hawk is one of my favorite winged creatures and appears to me at the most significant times, I decided one day to ask the universe to present me with a hawk feather as a token to keep of that beautiful animal. I figured that was small and easy enough since there were hawks in the area and one of them was bound to drop a feather or two (although I had never found one). Most of that summer, whenever I set out on my long morning walks, I looked for one. I found other feathers—blackbirds, blue jays, even cardinals. And when I returned from my walks, I would put them in a plate on the table in my entrance hall. The plate filled up, but not one hawk feather did I find. Still, I didn't give up so easily. I knew better than not to have faith.

One day, sometime in mid-August, I kayaked over to a small, unpopulated beach across the bay by my house. My favorite thing to do was to comb it for treasure, mainly shells and rocks. This time, though, instead of filling my bag with the usual riches, I stumbled upon feather after feather and decided to collect them instead. I found about 10 splendid and unique feathers in all! They were all shapes, colors and sizes. However, not one of them was a hawk feather. As I collected them I thought about my disappointment about not being able to find a single hawk feather among the many! Then, to my surprise, I found an entire bird wing. No bird attached, just the wing. It was clearly not a hawk wing, though. I had to laugh. Here, I was complaining about no hawk feather after being "gifted" all these wonderful feathers and now here was this wing full of feathers. It was as if the universe was telling me, "We gave you all these beautiful feathers and you still don't believe? What more do you want?" Well, I wanted the hawk feather.

The summer rolled on. Still nothing. In fact I pretty much forgot about it, even though in the back of my mind, I held on to the hope. Then one early September morning on my walk, I was overcome by a magnificent sunrise. Feeling ever so grateful, I took a few pictures. As I looked down at my phone to view the picture I just took, I noticed a majestic-looking black crow feather on the ground. I picked it up and carried it for the rest of my walk, feeling blessed with the nature that surrounded me. The next morning while walking, I again experienced a breathtaking sunrise. However, that particular morning I had a lot on my mind—an issue with my aging father, an upcoming trip where I had to go on a plane (something I hadn't done since before 9/11 and was terrified about), having to go back to work after a long summer vacation, a health issue I was having, and money problems my husband and I were facing. I stopped noticing the beauty around me because I became preoccupied with worry. I progressed to the point of worry where thoughts about all the worst things that could possibly happen in all those situations were taking over. I told myself I needed to stop worrying so much. But I couldn't stop. I just kept on walking and worrying, tuning out the beautiful world around me. Finally, I asked my higher power for help. I wanted to put an end to the horrible thoughts I was having and enjoy the beautiful morning like I had the day before. I wanted to be back in that place of positive energy and gratitude. It was at that very moment in prayer that I looked down. And there it was. Big and bold, right there in the street. The plain gray-white back side was face up. But as I picked it up and turned it *over, I saw the characteristic wavy stripes. The most exquisite hawk feather was right there in my hands. I couldn't believe what I was seeing. I spilled over with gratitude. So much so that my eyes welled up with tears. All my worries melted away. I knew at that moment that everything would be all right, no matter what the outcome.*

I keep that feather in a vase along with others I have collected (including other hawk ones I subsequently found). Every time I start to worry too much, I look at that particular one. Sometimes, I even hold it to feel the spirit of the hawk within me. It's a comforting reminder that the universe provides for us when we are in need and open to it. Sometimes instantly, sometimes at the precise moment when we need it most. In this case, after waiting an entire summer, there was no other moment that was more perfect.

Tuesday

Affirmations

Choose one, two, or all three of these affirmations to add to your daily affirmations and recite them each morning. Or write one of your own that affirms the benefits of time.

- Things happen when the time is right.
- I love the feeling of anticipating

something wonderful.

- I trust the universe has divine timing.

Wednesday

Active Practice

Notice synchronicities and celebrate them. You will be surprised at how often they occur. You may even want to keep a record of them. Keep in mind that nothing in the universe is a coincidence. Everything is orchestrated beautifully. It could be something as little as recognizing that you thought about someone and they called, to something as big as the house you have just been talking and dreaming about just went up for sale. Make sure you jot down some notes about it because you will be writing more fully about it later in the week. Take note of what you were feeling, thinking, or engaging in before the "coincidence" occurred.

Thursday

Active Practice

What are you anticipating? Is there something you have wanted and are waiting for it to happen? Is there a specific item that you have been wanting to get, such as a car, house, boat, or item of clothing? Have you been waiting for the right love relationship to enter your life? Do you feel like you have been waiting forever and you may never get it? Or are you waiting in joyful anticipation of it? Focus your thoughts on this thing that you're waiting for. Notice your feelings. If it gets you upset or makes you uncomfortable in any way to think about it, then chances are you have given up on the dream by throwing resistance onto your path. If the thought gives you tingles of delight, then you are well on your way to manifesting this very thing.

Keep your vibration up and it will come when the time is right.

Friday

Write About Your Journey

Keep a record of interesting synchronicities that have happened this week. Write down your feelings about each experience. What were you were feeling, thinking, or engaging in before the incident occurred?

Also write about anything you are anticipating and your feelings toward it. What are some ways you can change your attitude so that it can manifest even faster? List them.

Saturday and Sunday

Meditation

This sunrise meditation, *Rise*, reminds us that each day is a

Recordings of all the guided meditations, with music, are included with the purchase of this book. They can be accessed by going to www. harmonyspaces.net, and entering the access code CittaNadiROC. You can also scan the code at right with your phone.

new beginning and a new opportunity. Enjoy each moment in time as if it is the first moment the sun's rays and light touches the Earth. (Approximately 9 minutes)

Rise

Let's begin by finding your point of focus. It could be a steady noise in the room, a word that you repeat over and over, or your breath moving in and out.

Scan your body from feet to shoulders and neck and notice which muscles are tense. Relax and let go of the tension. Allow your body to feel open and balanced.

I'm going to guide you through a meditation ... a journey for your mind and spirit. If your mind wanders, or if unwanted thoughts creep in, just push them gently away and turn your attention back to my voice. If you are distracted by outside noises, try your best to ignore them, and again turn your attention back to my voice.

Let's begin.

The sun is rising, giving life to this new day.

As the sun's new rays reach out to the Earth and touch you, feel yourself absorbing its light. Allow your own light to shine. Begin at your heart center and let it radiate outward. Let your spirit glow with this light.

Feel the warmth of the new light of the sun. Allow it to penetrate every cell in your body. Keep very still as the warm rays fill every cell. Allow the warmth to circulate throughout your body. Let it move up and down and through every energy point. Now expand your aura and radiate that warmth to every living thing around you.

The rays of the sun are quiet but powerful. Feel its power. Feel your own quiet power within you. It is pulsating within you and without.

Bathe in the beauty of the sun's rays and colors. Find your beauty and color deep within you and allow it to shine like the sun. It is your own unique beauty like the uniqueness of each sunrise.

As you experience the beautiful energy of the sun, allow your heart to be filled with the love of the universe—the love of angels, spirit guides, your relatives and friends that are no longer here on earth, and all other beings that surround you with their love and light. Allow your heart to be filled with this love and bask in the joy that it brings you.

Begin this new day with joy. This is a clean slate, a chance to start anew. You can bring to this day anything you want. Bring happiness—happiness to yourself, and peace to others throughout this universe we share.

It is time for you to return to where you were when this meditation began. As I count backward from 5, slowly feel yourself come back to this room. 4 ... feel your legs and feet ... 3 ... feel the ground or chair beneath you ... 2 ... slowly move your arms and hands ... 1 ... take a deep breath and open your eyes when you are ready.

I have added this **Sun Gratitude Prayer** to uplift and inspire.

Father Sun, we are grateful for the nourishment that you provide for us and this earth. We thank you for your warm rays and the light that you give. We thank you for your beauty and brilliance, especially in the colors you create as you rise each day so majestically. We are grateful that we can rely on you and know you will always be there. Thank you for bringing us sunny day cheerfulness and for creating the clouds that will rain down on us so we may be clean and nourished. For your immense magnitude of power and energy, we are grateful.

Chapter Six

POSTULATE #6

Read and reflect

"A happy man is too satisfied with the present to dwell too much on the future."

—Albert Einstein

I was not surprised to discover that this quote illustrates Einstein's practice of what is commonly known as mindfulness. Mindfulness goes hand in hand with meditation and is a key element to becoming centered in mind and spirit. Mindfulness is defined as being fully present in the moment. It is thoroughly focusing your attention on what's currently happening. Einstein had an innate ability to do this. He never seemed to dwell on the past, nor did he worry about the future. He was fully engrossed in what he was doing or pondering in each moment. That incredible focus is what helped him to endure the mental capacity necessary to stick with a mathematical concept until it was worked out.

Albert Einstein had many challenges to overcome as a child and young adult. He was late in acquiring language as a youngster and had so much difficulty with it that there were suspicions that he would not be able to learn. On top of this, his teachers reported that he couldn't remember anything. He was able to compensate for these weaknesses as he progressed through school. However, as a young adult, he still met with roadblocks as he had a difficult time finding a job as a teaching professor, even in the university where he attended. After many rejections in this field, he finally found work as a third-class patent examiner instead. While others might develop a low self-esteem from these kind of challenges, none of these shortcomings seemed to affect Einstein. He didn't dwell on them. He didn't seem to worry about his future, either. He instead focused his attention on his studies and exhibited an unwavering immersion into his passions and interests (Churchill, S. 2018). Practicing mindfulness served him well.

W hy is mindfulness so essential to an aligned and happy life? There are quite a few benefits to moving through your days mindfully. Mindfulness allows you to be clear-minded. When your mind isn't cluttered with to-do lists, deadlines, past conversations, or activities, it allows you to make room for enriching ideas to flow. Using meditation to clear your mind and then focusing on the present makes way for clarity, allowing for inspirational thoughts to flood in. Perhaps this is how Einstein was able to work out all those complicated math equations!

Being mindful also helps you appreciate what you are doing. If you make it a point to be fully aware and approach each task with gratitude, this will most definitely lead to a feeling of happiness. Try it sometime. Focus on each activity you undertake and practice appreciating it as you are carrying it out. Note how quickly your mood lifts even when it's something you don't like doing. One morning, I set aside the entire day to work on this very chapter. However, as I sat down to write, my daughter called and said she was having trouble with her car and needed me to pick her up from her apartment and drive her to an appointment. I was annoyed that I had to take a significant amount of time out to help her when I had dedicated the day to writing. But my daughter needed me and I wasn't about to let her down. I could have spent the ride to her place moaning and complaining about what I perceived to be an inconvenience. Instead, I shifted my mindset and decided to practice mindful appreciation for these new circumstances. I had just downloaded a few new songs, so I was happy to have the chance to listen to them on the way. I was able to be fully present for my daughter as we drove to her appointment. She and I ended up conversing, laughing, and thoroughly enjoying each other's company. What started out to be a stressful situation for both of us became a pleasant morning where we both succumbed to just being in the moment. I was truly grateful for the precious time spent with her. (Interesting how this situation occurred just as I was writing this chapter. Another synchronicity!)

Staying focused in the moment also allows you to achieve success. I am fairly certain that Einstein did not allow outside influences to take his focus away from whatever mathematical or physical conundrum he happened to be working on at the time. He was one who was known to persevere until he achieved the solutions he was seeking.

Practicing mindfulness is also helpful for coping with worrisome thoughts, feelings, and body sensations. Being mindful of them without judgement or worry gives you the ability to accept them, causing you to feel more calm and easy. Sometimes trying to ignore a nagging thought or pain can lead to more discomfort or foul moods. Turning toward the pain or discomfort and acknowledging it helps you to face it, know it, and understand it. This gives you a sense of calm about it. It puts you in a position of power where you can choose how you are going to react to it. There is less of a chance you will be carried away by your thoughts. You will be able to look at them objectively and will be less likely to obsess over them or beat yourself up for having them.

Mindfulness is also beneficial when you're trying to make a decision about something in that it allows a greater capacity of appropriate solutions to come through. Again, focusing on the moment helps to empty the mind of all unnecessary thoughts and allows for clear thinking. To your pleasant surprise, that decision you have been struggling with will suddenly become a no-brainer. Practice mindfulness on a daily basis, and decisions in general will become easier, requiring little effort.

Tuesday

Affirmations

Choose any or all of these affirmations to add to your daily affirmations and recite them each morning. Or write one of your own that affirms the joy of being in the moment.

- I appreciate each moment of every day.
- I am in the moment.
- Having a clear mind allows inspirations and ideas to come through.
- I acknowledge my feelings and body sensations without judgment or worry.

Wed'nesday

Active Practice

We touched upon mindfulness in Chapter One, where we practiced using our different senses to appreciate the little miracles of life. Now I'm going to present a bit of a challenge.

Every day we all have to experience unpleasant tasks that we don't like to engage in. Whether it is folding laundry, going to work or school, driving our kids around, or visiting the doctor or dentist, there are just certain things that we consider a chore or bothersome.

Your practice is to choose an unpleasant task and carry it out mindfully. Find something about it that you appreciate and revel in that feeling of gratitude. For example, if you are having a checkup at the dentist, focus on how clean your mouth is going to feel. Appreciate the feeling of the water washing away all the unwanted stains and crud and the polish making your teeth shiny and whiter.

Notice the tastes, smells, and sensations (unless, of course, they are extremely unpleasant, in which case it would be best to distract yourself from them!). Practice a feeling of gratitude for the hygienist working hard to help you feel clean and fresh and good when you smile. Note how the experience is different than usual and how you feel afterward.

Thursday

Active Practice

Engage in a mindful interaction with someone. Have a conversation with a friend, family member, or colleague and remain fully focused on them and what they are saying. Stay in the moment, and appreciate this person's knowledge, opinions, point of view, and curiosities. Try to push away any judgments you have and ignore the tendency to formulate a response or opinion as they are talking. Basically, be a good listener without injecting your two cents, and note how and where the conversation goes. Also, be mindful of how the other person receives you.

Friday

Write About Your Journey

Journal about your feelings regarding your mindful task, conversation, or both. Here are some questions to ponder: How did you feel? Was it difficult to stay focused? Did you find the unpleasant task to be more tolerable or even somewhat enjoyable? How did your feelings change, if at all, about the person you were conversing with? Did you feel more present and alive during these mindful activities? Did you feel happy or experience any other emotions?

Saturday and Sunday

Meditation

This is the only meditation in the book that is self-guided. It is a walking meditation. (Duration: You set the time.)

Take a mindful walk. Be aware of all you are sensing; sounds, sights, smells. Be aware of the sun on your face, the breeze in your hair, or raindrops on your nose! If your mind wanders, turn your focus back to your surroundings. A place where nature is abundant like a wooded area, beach, lake or mountain trail, would be a great setting for this walking meditation.

If you can't be outside, take a gratitude walk inside. Walk around your house, office, or other indoor space, and with each step think of something you are grateful for. You can also do this while walking around a labyrinth if you have access to one nearby.

Chapter Seven

POSTULATE #7

Read and reflect

"The intuitive mind is a sacred gift and the rational mind is a faithful servant. We have created a society that honors the servant and forgotten the gift."

—Albert Einstein

No one had a more well-developed logical mind than Albert Einstein. Yet he saw the benefit in remembering, honoring, developing, and trusting the gift of intuition. How could someone so well-versed in left-brain notions such as math and the sciences understand the value of the intuitive spirit? Perhaps it's because without it, he would not have been able to open his mind to allow his deep understanding and knowledge to flow through him.

Einstein says the rational mind is a faithful servant, but now I'm posing this question: Is the rational mind a servant to us, or are we a servant to it?

Do we as a society rely too much on rationality? There's a stigma about intuition that has made it unworthy of acknowledgment in this day and age. It holds labels such as *mythical*, *paranormal*, *unaccountable*, *occult*, *abstract*, *obscure*, *recondite*, or *arcane*. To the rational-minded person, these labels aren't necessarily positive. But have we done ourselves a disservice by ignoring our innate knowledge? What about this idea of inspired, intuitive thoughts becoming manifestations of physical things or proven ideas? Did Einstein's brilliance come from his ability to tap into his higher intelligence through his intuitive nature?

Napoleon Hill wrote the following in his book *Think and Grow Rich*: "Through the faculty of creative imagination, the finite mind of man has direct communication with Infinite Intelligence. It is the faculty through which 'hunches' and 'inspirations' are received. It is by this faculty that all basic, or new ideas are handed over to man" (Hill, 2013). It is true that Thomas Edison used his rational mind to "try out" thousands of ideas before he "tuned in" to his creative mind, his intuition, and was able to perfect the incandescent light and "talking machine." Dr. Elmer R. Gates is not well-known but is responsible for hundreds of patents, including the foam fire extinguisher, an improved electric iron, and a climate-controlled air conditioner. He discovered what he called *psychotaxis*, which basically entailed turning thoughts into things. His method involved focusing on what is already known, and by doing this intensely, he would bring about associations and connections of the "subconscious" to images, concepts, ideas, and thoughts, thus resulting in new insights about the subject (Humphries, 2006-08). I call that intuition leading to manifestation. The universal Law of Attraction strikes again!

There have been too many times where people have had outlandish ideas and then dismissed them because they thought they were crazy. Meanwhile, the most brilliant inventions and theories have been born from out-of-the-box thinking. Just think of what this world would be like without the imagination of Albert Einstein. How about Edison, Franklin, Van Gogh, Emerson, Carnegie, Gates, Jobs, and countless others? Not only did they develop innovative ideas, but they also had the courage to follow through with them. They wouldn't have seen their notions through without some kind of intuition, some kind of inner intelligence that they perceived and acknowledged.

Where would the world be today if Einstein wasn't driven by his inspirations? What would have happened if he just sat in his room and merely entertained his ideas about energy, matter, and the speed of light, and instead conceded to other mundane or even worrisome thoughts that otherwise occupied and cluttered his mind? Einstein knew the value of intuitive thinking. His intelligence flowed through him with ease as he allowed his inspirations to expand and extend to places far beyond his imagination.

There's something to be said about trusting our intuition not only to allow brilliant ideas to flow but also to guide us through life. How many times has our intuition worked for us yet we refuse to admit that is the case? I'm sure you have heard stories about situations where people have made decisions based on a hunch or feeling. Have you ever been thinking about someone and decided to call them only to find out they have been thinking about you or had some big news? Or have you ever felt the urge to take a different route to work one day only to find out there was a terrible accident on your usual route? We dismiss these stories as coincidences, but are they really? After the 9/11 attacks on New York City in 2001, I heard stories about how people acted on an impulse not to go to work that day or for unknown reasons decided to go in late. There were numerous accounts of people who just had a feeling they should stay home or were driven to leave the building before it collapsed. One such story involved a woman named Greer Epstein. She was an executive director at Morgan Stanley in the World Trade Center. She was known to never take any kind of break from work. But shortly before the first plane hit, Greer decided uncharacteristically to take a cigarette break with a friend. She ignored the jolt she felt in the elevator going down only to find herself standing outside minutes later, watching the inferno that ensued after first plane went right through the floor where her office was located (Park, 2011). Then there's the story of Michael Moy, a software engineer for IQ Financial Inc. After the first plane hit, he decided not to listen to the announcements to remain in his office on the 83rd floor and persuaded some co-workers to instead head down the stairs with him. Had he not followed his intuition, he and his co-workers would have perished when the building crashed down (Tomsho, Carton, & Guidera, 2001).

There are similar documented accounts of people who decided not to board the Titanic on that fateful trip in 1912 or relatives of passengers having "premonitions" about the disaster. One such passenger, Norman Craig, a Scottish MP and king's counsel, decided last minute not to board the Titanic. He later wrote about it: "I suddenly decided not to sail, I cannot tell you why; there was simply no reason for it. I had no mysterious premonitions or visions of any kind nor did I dream of any disaster. But I do know that, at practically the last moment, I did not want to go" (Weidbinger, 2011). It's interesting how when people listen to their hearts, major outcomes happen as a result.

The logical mind is valuable, but never underestimate or dismiss your inner voice. It could offer itself as a thought, a feeling, an idea, or an inspiration. It could steer you in the direction of a life-altering event or help you make everyday decisions that are in your best interest.

Just recently, my husband and two kids decided to go on vacation across the country to a family wedding. Although I usually jump at the chance of vacationing with my family, as it's rare that we get to spend time together, for some reason I was not feeling good about going away at this particular time. Our family dog, Naya, was showing signs of her age, and I was feeling uncomfortable about leaving her with someone. I had a nagging feeling, as if my intuition was telling me a major event was going to happen with her soon. In addition, I was scheduled to deliver a major presentation close to the time we would be away, and I didn't want flight issues or any other kind of delays to threaten my chances of getting to my presentation on time. So I stayed home while my family flew off to Arizona. The weekend before they were to leave, Naya had a major seizure resulting from a stroke. She was in the hospital for a couple of days and was unable to stand up and walk. We were faced with the decision of whether to end her life here on earth. My husband, son, and I went to the hospital first, and my daughter was to meet us there. We were put in a private room with our family pet of 14 ½ years. You can imagine the emotion we were experiencing as we sat with her, coming to the realization that these would be our last moments with her. Not long after, my daughter arrived. She has always had a very special connection with Naya and as soon as she entered the room, the old girl perked up. My adult daughter embraced her with happiness and joy of a 10-year-old. Realizing the rest of us had been crying, she said, "Why is everyone crying? There is no reason for tears. We are bringing this puppy home and everything is going to be OK." How could she be so sure? Perhaps it was her connection to this animal, or perhaps it was her connection to the divine, or both, but she just intuitively knew it wasn't Naya's time. A long discussion ensued with a lot of emotion, and in the end we took our baby home. The next day, Naya began walking. And by the time my family returned from their vacation, I had nursed her back to her old (and I mean old!) self, and she went on to live another seven months.

My intuition told me not to leave Naya, and my daughter's intuition told her our old girl was going to be all right. Had we not listened, things most likely would have turned out very differently. In both cases, we were each led by our inner guidance.

We have all had such experiences. As I reflect on the time when my husband and I were looking for our first house together, I recall visiting many different places and not feeling good about any. But when we walked into the one that we eventually did buy, we both knew it was the one. There was just a feeling of pleasure and comfort. Like we were home. I distinctly remember going out on the deck. It was unusually warm for February, and the sun was shining brightly. I heard my inner voice say, "This is it," and I felt excitement well up in me. The same went for when my son and I were looking at colleges. He knew he loved his college of choice the minute he stepped on campus. Again the words "this is it" were spoken by him.

Don't discount your intuition. It is very powerful and will become more unclouded as you practice the tools laid out in this book. Becoming aligned with that divine part of you will help you to open up to its voice. It can inspire great ideas and help you to make choices that affect yourself and others in a positive way. Nothing bad ever comes out of listening to your own inner voice. It comes from a place of wisdom and clarity. It is of divine spirit and knows exactly what you want and what is best. Your inner self always knows the easiest path to get to what you desire. It is up to you to listen and find your way to it. Once you allow yourself to see the path open up for you, you will be surprised by how everything falls right along into place.

How do you listen and allow your intuition to flow through you? Begin by following the processes that have been laid out here in Postulates 1, 2 and 3; the practices of gratitude and appreciation, meditation, and communing with nature. If you do just these three things each day, your mind will be clear, opening up a channel directly to your inner voice. Because when you are relaxed and free of discord, intuition is at its best. You will know you are on the right path when you feel inspired. Ideas will begin to flow, which influence other ideas and events to happen, which can lead to you getting that promotion, that new job, that lover that is just right for you, or that house you have been dreaming about. You have already learned that your ideas about everything are born out of your thoughts. Your thinking is best inspired when you are closest to your higher self. That is when your intuition is at its peak. Learn to listen and follow it, and your urges to take action. It will speak to you in straightforward, plain language. You will know exactly what action to take because you will feel a strong impulse to do so. And you will know that it's right because of your gratifying feeling about it.

Tuesday

Affirmations

Choose any or all of these affirmations to add to your daily list and recite them each morning. Or write one of your own that affirms the gift of intuition.

- I trust my intuition and follow it, knowing it will lead me to the best possible outcome.
- My inner guidance knows what's best for me.
- I listen to the voice of my heart and spirit.

Wednesday

Active Practice

Practice using your intuition to make simple decisions. Get in a quiet place, relax your mind and body, and focus on an easy decision you have to make—such as what to have for lunch or which handbag to buy. Make it a simple decision that has only two options. Focus on your feelings about each and learn how your inner wisdom communicates with you. Perhaps you have an inner voice that talks to you, or you might get some mental images. Or perhaps you might just get physical sensations in your body or emotional feelings. Pay attention and see what happens. And then follow the flow and make your choice.

There's no right or wrong in this exercise. It's simply to help you figure out how your inner being feeds you wisdom about any given subject of focus.

Thursday

Active Practice

Think about times when your intuition served you. Have there ever been times when you were steered in the direction of something by your thoughts or feelings and it was the right path? What part did your intuition play in making major decisions? Did you always listen? What happened when you didn't listen to the voice of your heart? Have you ever been steered away from something? How many times did you just know not to take a certain route in your car and found out later there was an accident or traffic? Or perhaps you avoided a major event like the attacks on 9/11. Reflect and be grateful for the times you listened and followed your inner voice.

Friday

Write About Your Journey

Write a story about a time you listened to your intuition and how it served you. How would things have been different had you not followed your instinct? Is there anything you would do differently?

Saturday and Sunday

Meditation

Recordings of all the guided meditations, with music, are included with the purchase of this book. They can be accessed by going to www. harmonyspaces.net, and entering the access code CittaNadiROC. You can also scan the code at right with your phone.

This is a simple meditation to help you clear your mind so that you can be open to your inner wisdom speaking to you. It will also guide you in learning how to find your point of focus when meditating on your own in silence. (Duration: approximately 10 minutes.)

Let's begin by finding your point of focus. It could be a steady noise in the room, a word that you repeat over and over like om, or love, or calm. Or your breath moving in and out.

Scan your body from your feet to your shoulders and neck and notice which muscles are tense. Relax and let go of the tension. Allow your body to feel tuned in, open, and balanced.

I am now going to guide you through a meditation ... a journey for your mind and spirit. If your mind wanders, or if unwanted thoughts make their way in, just push them gently away and turn your attention back to my voice. If you are distracted by outside noises, try your best to ignore them, and again turn your attention back to my voice.

Ready? Let us begin.

I want you to imagine you have a root, like a tree root, extending out of your bottom and making its way all the way down into the deepest part of the earth. Let it reach the Earth's fiery core. Now I want you to send love from your heart down that root into the Earth with gratitude for all she provides for you. Tune into the feeling of love surging up this root back to your heart. This is the Earth returning her love back to you. Feel its energy spread throughout your body and spirit. Sit for a minute and bathe in that love energy.

Clear your mind of all thought.

Imagine your thoughts fading away, like a whisper.

You are left with a blank, wide-open space.

Sit in the stillness and serenity.

Transcend into the stillness and peace that is your soul.

Continue to quiet your mind to allow the messages of your inner voice to come through.

The love of the universe is flowing through and around you. Its tremendous power is always with you, always surrounding you, and ready to uplift you to your highest potential.

Know that the universe's eternal love is always here, always with you. You can tap into it at any time by just quieting your mind and listening to your spirit's voice.

Listen now and allow its message to flow through you.

(Allow 2 minutes.)

It is time for you to return to where you were when this meditation began. As I count backward from 5, slowly feel yourself come back to this room. 4 … feel your legs and feet … 3 … feel the ground or chair beneath you … 2 … slowly move your arms and hands … 1 … take a deep breath and open your eyes when you are ready.

Chapter Eight

POSTULATE #8

Read and reflect

<hr/>

"Try not to become a man of success but a man of value."

—*Albert Einstein*

What did Einstein mean by success in this quote? Someone who makes good money? Is married and has children to carry on the family name? A person who has a respectable job, a nice place to live, and many friends?

What is your idea of success? Think about it carefully.

I believe that a man or woman of value *is* a person of success. If that's the case, then, what can we say about the meaning of the word *value*? I can only speculate what

Einstein meant. He could have meant someone who is worth a lot of money. My heart tells me that is not the case, though. I believe what he meant by a person that is of value is a person who *has* values. Moral standards that he lives by. All people I know that are spiritually aligned have some kind of moral values. There are many sets of standards that might be considered to be moral in nature. I am going to focus on three that I feel are common to spiritually healthy people.

The Givers

Earlier I referred to Lao Tzu's writings in the Tou Te Ching about the four virtues to live by. No. 4 refers to **Supportiveness—service** to others without expectation of reward (Tzu, 2015).

There are those people who are very generous and giving of themselves. Do you know someone like this? They are the ones who are always lending a helping hand, who genuinely care about what's going on in your life, and who give generously of their love. They are the gift givers. They are the ones who give their time volunteering for a cause they feel strongly about. They're the people who others refer to as the ones who would "give you the shirt off their back." You probably know at least one person like this. Do you have that person in mind? Think about him or her for a minute. Is this person always happy? Chances are she is because it feels good to give and to help others. And you've heard it said that when you give, you receive so much more in return. This is true, but be careful not to be a giving person just for the purpose of getting something in return.

There are those such people who pose as givers but really have another agenda in mind. They are the ones who do good deeds or act concerned for reasons other than to serve. They are always looking for a pat on the back for their acts of kindness and perform good deeds for that reason only. They are the ones asking "what's in it for me?" and always looking for their kudos. When they ask a question seemingly out of concern, they are usually looking for information from you to compare with their own situation. They are eager to compliment in order to "buy" your friendship.

On the surface these people seem kind and caring, and perhaps their acts are helpful to others. If you recognize yourself in this description, there's a good chance you are not fundamentally happy. You might find yourself on a constant quest for happiness and are frustrated when you can't find it. The good news is, it is not too difficult to change. All you have to do is change one simple question. Instead of asking "What will I get out of this?" ask "How may I serve others?" It doesn't have to take a colossal act. Small acts of kindness such as reading to an elderly person in your neighborhood or picking up garbage on your local beach or park is a great way to start to make a difference. You will feel good, maybe even connect with people in a loving and special way. And that's kudos enough, don't you think?

Every week at my place of employment, we have a box in the main office labeled "Friday Fortune." If we want, we can place a dollar with our name on it in the box. A dollar is drawn on Fridays, and whoever's name is on that dollar wins the entire pot! One day I decided that every week, in addition to my own name, I would submit a second dollar with the name of a friend on it. I thought, "Wouldn't that be fun if my friend's name was drawn?" And only I would know! Well, after three weeks of doing that my own name was drawn and I won $50. My act of giving attracted an act of receiving.

I have a friend whose name gets drawn often. She is one of those people who are always giving of themselves, and she is very well liked by everyone around her. I recently found out she donates the money to charity every time she wins. Now that's beautiful!

Don't make it a point to give only so that you can receive in return. Give for the sake of serving others, and in doing so, you will receive the fullness of who you are and find happiness.

The Owners

A person of value is one who takes responsibility for

himself and his own life circumstances. This is a very rare find, which is why it holds value. Think about all the times things weren't going well in your life. How many times did you blame another? Did you blame your spouse, mother, general upbringing, or friend for your unhappiness or negative circumstances in your life? A person who is spiritually aligned blames less and takes responsibility for his own life. While your mother might be the reason you have a phobia of heights, it is up to you to continue with this phobia and take responsibility or to do something about it instead of blaming her for the rest of your life. While you may be in a financial bind because your ex-spouse spent all your money on gambling, drinking, or drugs, it is up to you to continue blaming him and acting as a victim or pick yourself up and start again. No matter how old you are, or whatever the circumstances, you can take charge of your life. Spending your days blaming and resenting is not beneficial to you. It only increases your resentment and makes you feel worse. You can choose to be miserable, or you can choose happiness. Even in the worst of circumstances, you can choose how you react to any situation. You are in total control of how you decide to feel. You can be scared and worried, or you can be hopeful. You can be angry and vengeful, or you can be forgiving. You can be bitter and resentful, or you can surrender those feelings and choose freedom. It is always up to you. A person who adopts the better-feeling emotion is usually the happiest, no matter what the situation is. This makes him or her a person of value.

The Compassionate

Lao Tzu's third cardinal virtue is **Gentleness**, a sense of **kindness** to each other and every living thing and a sensitivity to spiritual truth (Tzu, 2015).

Showing kindness to others is a valuable trait, and if practiced on a regular basis it can make you stand out and shine. It isn't all that difficult to be kind even if you are in conflict with someone. If you can get out of your own way a little bit and replace the need to be right with the desire to be kind, you will find that conflicts carry less of a toll and are more easily resolved. This is not a suggestion to let people walk all over you but an approach that allows you to view conflicts with compassion for the other parties involved and try to come to some kind of resolution rather than pushing against them to get your point heard.

You might think this is easier said than done, but only if you don't give it a try. Here is a story to illustrate this point.

> *Sylvia and Ron have been married for 10 years and have been fighting for the last six months. Ron has been accusing Sylvia of*

having an ongoing affair at work with another man whom she insists is only a friend. For months, she has been digging in her heels, trying everything she can to convince Ron he is wrong. She is involved in a particular project with this man and has had to spend a good amount of time with him, but it's all work-related. Ron wants to believe her but has a difficult time when he hears about the lunch meetings they attend together, the time spent after-hours and the weekend phone calls. On the days Sylvia stays late, Ron stews as he imagines all types of scenarios going on while he eats a microwave dinner in front of the TV. This has dominated all their conversations, and they are even talking divorce.

One day, Sylvia decides to take a different approach. She sits down with Ron and really listens to what he is saying. She makes it a point to just hear him with compassion and an open heart. She realizes how much he was suffering. What she hears when she listens with compassion is simply that Ron misses her and feels neglected. He resents the other man for having the opportunity to spend so much time on something important with his wife. And it takes away precious time he could be spending with her. Sylvia comes to the conclusion that *her husband really doesn't believe she is having an affair. It is just difficult for him to see her spending so much time with this man on this project. Once Sylvia can really sympathize with her husband, she softens her stance and acts in kindness instead. She adjusted her schedule. She tries her best to be home at a certain hour, and once a week she prepares Ron's favorite meal. She still has to attend lunch meetings with her work partner, but she makes sure she calls or texts Ron once a day just to check in to see how his day was going. This way he knows she is thinking about him. On the weekends, Ron and Sylvia make sure they set aside a couple of hours just for them. Both their phones are shut off and they don't talk about work. Eventually, Ron takes more of an interest in Sylvia's work project. He asks questions and finds himself hoping for a positive outcome for her.*

When viewed with compassion and kindness on both ends, this situation is resolved. Sylvia is able to complete the project successfully, and Ron is rooting for her the entire way.

They both benefit monetarily, which ends up being more than they expected!

Tuesday

Affirmations

Choose any or all of these affirmations to add to your daily affirmations and recite them each morning. Or write one of your own that affirms that you are a person of value.

- I choose kindness and compassion over blame or resentment.
- I live life with kindness and compassion in my heart.
- I am loved and I love others.
- I have value and worth.

Wednesday

Active Practice

Be a person of value. Perform a random act of kindness for someone else. It could be for a stranger or loved one. Here are some ideas:

- If you are going through the cash line at a toll booth, pay the toll of the person behind you.
- Spend time making a favorite dessert for a loved one and surprise him or her with it.
- Visit with an elderly person in your neighborhood.

Read to that person, or just sit and listen.

- Leave someone a small gift in the mailbox or on the doorstep: store coupons, inspiring quotes, lottery ticket, brownies, or flowers.
- Help someone shovel snow off the driveway, clean leaves off the lawn or debris from the sidewalk in front of the house.
- Pay for someone's coffee at your local café.
- Bring a hot beverage or cold drink to someone who works outside in all weather conditions, such as a sanitation worker, crossing guard, or landscaper.
- Offer to sit with a pet, child, or elderly parent to allow someone to run errands or go on a date.
- Make a care package for a homeless person or veteran.
- Tell someone what you appreciate about her. This kind of compliment can make someone's day.
- Put a loving note in your child's lunchbox or your spouse's briefcase or planner.
- Show your appreciation to someone who helped you at the store or with a service by putting a good word in with that person's supervisor.

Thursday

Active Practice

If you find yourself in conflict with someone, try to approach the situation with kindness and compassion rather than trying to prove you're right. Step into his shoes and see his point of view. Notice how the dynamics of the interaction change and how powerful you can be to soften the conflict. You have the power to change something that could have blown up into something stressful to defusing it right on the spot and moving on.

Friday

Write About Your Journey

Write about your random act of kindness. What did you do? How did it feel to see the joy or appreciation in the person for whom you were performing it? What other ideas do you have for these kinds of acts?

Saturday and Sunday

Meditation

Loving Kindness (Metta) meditation: This is the meditation spoken about earlier in Chapter 4. It directs loving kindness to yourself and to others. (Duration: approximately 5 minutes.)

Let's begin by finding your point of focus. It could be a steady noise in the room, a word that you repeat over and over, or your breath moving in and out.

Scan your body from feet to shoulders and neck and

Recordings of all the guided meditations, with music, are included with the purchase of this book. They can be accessed by going to www. harmonyspaces.net, and entering the access code CittaNadiROC. You can also scan the code at right with your phone.

notice which muscles are tense. Relax and let go of the tension. Allow your body to feel open and balanced.

I'm going to guide you through a meditation ... a journey for your mind and spirit. If your mind wanders, or if unwanted thoughts creep in, just push them gently away and turn your attention back to my voice. If you are distracted by outside noises, try your best to ignore them, and again turn your attention back to my voice.

Ready? Let's begin.

(Think about yourself and your well-being.)
May I be calm.
May I be healthy and strong.
May I have peace.

(Bring to mind someone you love.)
May you be calm.
May you be healthy and strong.
May you have peace.

(Bring to mind someone you don't know very well.)

May you be calm.
May you be healthy and strong.
May you have peace.

(Bring to mind someone with whom you are having a conflict.)
May you be calm.
May you be healthy and strong.
May you have peace.

(Bring to mind everyone in your circle.)
May we be calm.
May we be healthy and strong.
May we have peace.

(Send out to the entire universe.)
May all beings everywhere be calm.
May all beings everywhere be healthy and strong.
May all beings everywhere have peace.

It is time for you to return to where you were when this meditation began. As I count backward from 5, slowly feel yourself come back to this room. 4 ... feel your legs and feet ... 3 ... feel the ground or chair beneath you ... 2 ... slowly move your arms and hands ... 1 ... take a deep breath and open your eyes when you are ready.

Chapter Nine

POSTULATE #9

Read and reflect

"A clever person solves a problem.
A wise person avoids it."

—*Albert Einstein*

Perhaps this was Albert Einstein's humorous way of reminding us to go about life cautiously and mindfully, so as to avoid problems. But I choose to interpret this quote a little differently. As stated earlier, I believe conflict is good. It helps us to decipher and make clear our desires. If we remain with the attitude that conflict is good, and we don't become stuck in a loop of focusing on it, we will benefit.

When I was a little girl, if I complained about a headache, my dad would lovingly say, "How about I step on your foot so you forget about your headache?" OK, so focusing on another problem to avoid the first one is not quite the answer, either. But I feel it is along those lines that this quote is pointed.

How does one avoid a potential problem? The answer is simple: by not focusing on it or shifting your attention to something else.

Perhaps we can turn from one physicist to another to help accentuate this point.

Sir Isaac Newton and his 3 Laws of Motion

Newton put into words and equations the Laws of Motion. The first states in simple terms that *an object at rest will remain at rest unless acted on by an unbalanced force. An object in motion continues in motion with the same speed and in the same direction unless acted upon by an unbalanced force*. The same goes for the energy of thoughts. If you keep focusing your thoughts on a potential problem (focus=the force), it gains momentum and grows bigger and bigger. If you don't give a potential problem any attention, and let it lie dormant, it will remain at rest. This is how I choose to interpret Einstein's ideas about avoiding a problem.

The first part of Newton's second Law of Motion

begins like this: ***Acceleration is produced when a force acts on a mass***. Again, the same goes for thought energy. When you begin to focus your thoughts (the force), on a potential issue, it will begin to accelerate.

If you have already started the motion, and the problem begins to gain momentum, then take your focus off the issue and put it on the solution. This brings us to Newton's third law of motion: ***For every action there is an equal and opposite reaction***. For every problem, there is a solution.

How to grow a problem

Imagine you come across a problem. Let's liken it to a spark or small fire. Every time you put on a log, it fuels the fire and makes it bigger. Think about how whenever you think another thought about a potential problem, it's like putting another log on the fire. Now imagine what happens when you throw water or sand on the fire. It extinguishes it.

If you continue to think about an issue, it has the potential for turning into a problem, from spark to fire. It starts with the news of the issue. It could be something getting in the way of you achieving a goal, a conflict with another, a malfunction of some kind, or an illness. As soon as you give it your attention, you are giving it acceleration. Now you begin to focus on the issue at hand with anger, mistrust, sadness, or defeat. You complain about it to everyone you know, you obsess about it day and night, and you write about how it's ruining your life. It is the last thing you think about at night and the first thing you focus on when you get up in the morning. This is when the problem begins to take on momentum. After a while, you are on an endless loop of turning this problem over and over in your mind and dwelling on all the ways it is causing you distress. And soon, what started out at zero motion is moving at an unbelievable speed. Why? Because you have applied the force. You have fed and nourished it by thinking about all the ways this problem is affecting your life. You have thrown more logs on the fire. Thinking of all the other potential problems that can arise or have already been spawned, or yelling, screaming, and crying over it will only feed it more.

Now let's bring in another universal law: the Law of Attraction. Remember, this law states that wherever your thoughts are focused, this is what will be attracted into your life. If you are unhappy with your current living situation and are focusing on that while feeling bad about it, you will only attract more of the same situation. This is because the lack of what you want is where your focus is. Think about that for a minute. If the LACK of what you want is where you are focusing your thoughts, you will experience more lack! If you keep focusing on the same problem, more problems like that will come into your experience. In fact, you might notice that the same issues do keep occurring over and over. And when that happens long enough, you may become convinced that the same recurring issue will be a thorn in your side forever. If this is what you believe, then it will be, because the universe delivers everything that matches your vibrational stance. If there is a problem that keeps popping up, and you expect that it will keep showing up, or you keep talking about it, then the Law of Attraction will make sure it continues to appear and reappear. It's just the way the law works. You keep attracting it, it keeps showing up. Simple as that.

How to squash a problem before it gains momentum

You get bad news or come upon an unpleasant situation. You begin to focus on the solution with kindness, positivity, hope, or expectation. You keep focusing on solutions rather than on the problem, and you keep your spirits up. Pretty soon, the problem diminishes and you are no worse off. So basically you have just avoided the problem. It's like throwing dirt on the fire while it is still small.

We just learned that an issue becomes a problem with focus. Therefore, the way to avoid a problem is to not focus on the issue but rather allow it to lie dormant. But avoidance isn't always the outcome you want; it often just defers the ultimate action. So you then turn your focus to the positive outcome: the solution.

- I will figure this out.
- I can take a break from this, find alignment with myself by meditating and clearing my mind, and then come back to it with a different perspective and focus.
- I believe that there is a solution to this problem.
- This is not as bad as I have been making it out to be.

Sounds easy enough. But what happens if you have already allowed the problem to grow and it becomes an even bigger problem? Now what? There still may be time to minimize it or at least stop it in its tracks. You can begin by noticing that you have allowed it to manifest into an issue.

I have allowed this problem to get out of hand.

Try not to place negative judgment on yourself. This happens to everybody. Pat yourself on the back for recognizing it and doing something about it. And note that it's not too late to turn the problem around or at least diminish it.

I can't control this situation, but I do

> have control over how I react from here
> on. I am not going to give this problem
> any more focused attention.

Once you stop focusing on the problem and shift your attention, it will stop hijacking your thoughts, and you can make room for a solution to come to you. Or it may simply go away on its own.

One way to stop focusing on an issue is to surrender and put it in the hands of God or the Universe, then let it go. By surrendering it to the higher power you stop giving it attention, you slow the momentum, and you can allow solutions to be brought to light.

Is it really that easy to let something go? It might seem like a quick, easy solution. However, in reality, how do you let go of an issue that is prevalent in your everyday experience? It's easy to let go of a heavy weight you are physically carrying. You just drop it and instantly feel relief. But how do you release a problem that you keep thinking about? Especially one that seemingly keeps gnawing at you day and night? Believe it or not, you do have control. Even when something antagonistic is consuming your thoughts. A thought is a vibration, and as easily as you acquire it, you can relinquish it.

Here's a simple tactic that I teach my meditation classes.

Remember to **B.R.E.A.T.H.E.** This is a simple acronym that you can use to help release a negative thought pattern.

B.R.E.A.T.H.E.

B is for **Breathing**. Use a breathing exercise to calm your body and mind. Simply take a few deep, cleansing breaths right down into your belly and begin the process of clearing your mind.

RE is for **Relax your muscles**. Take an inventory of your muscles and note which ones are tensed up. Then systematically relax each one.

A is for **Attitude**. Move gently from an attitude of negativity to one of general positivity and trust.

TH is for **Thoughts**. And **E**, for **Emotions**. Change your thoughts and emotions about the subject. Now this doesn't mean that you think the opposite thought. It should be one that is believable and one that eases you out of your bad feeling.

For example, if your issue is that you have gained weight and you have the constant negative thought of *I am fat*, changing that thought to *I am thin* or *I look beautiful just the way I am* is probably not going to make you feel better because you may not be ready to believe it. Choosing a thought such as *I can begin exercising and making healthy food choices today, and in the meantime I can wear clothes that are flattering to the way my body looks right now* will ease you gently out of the unpleasant emotion and negative self-talk. It is more believable.

Remembering to **B.R.E.A.T.H.E.** is a good strategy to help you break out of an adverse thought pattern and stop the momentum.

Tuesday

Affirmations

Choose any or all of these affirmations to add to your daily affirmations and recite them each morning. Or write one of your own affirming that you can keep problems from growing.

- I pause when I begin to focus too much on something unwanted.
- I am solution-oriented.
- I avoid problems by not giving them too much attention.
- I can choose how I react to any situation.

Wednesday

Active Practice

Take note of how many times a day you notice a potential problem and begin to focus your thoughts around it. It could be about something as little as your coffee wasn't hot enough. Notice how it begins to "snowball" from there. You might spill it on yourself, or you are fumbling for your keys when you get back to your car and drop it. Are you deciding that it's going to be a bad day and expecting more debacles that will most likely come your way? Or are you laughing it off and telling yourself it's OK followed by more soothing thoughts? Take note of what happens as a result of your attitude.

Thursday

Active Practice

Take the analogy of kicking dirt on a fire and apply it to a problem you are facing. As you apply soothing thoughts, visualize yourself throwing dirt onto the fire. Use the B.R.E.A.T.H.E acronym. Remember, soothing thoughts are not just any positive thoughts that are the opposite of what you are feeling. Those might tend to make you feel worse. Soothing thoughts are general positive thoughts that ease your feelings about the situation. Here are some suggestions for general statements you can make to yourself:

- I have been in situations like this before and have always come out of them OK.
- I can come back to this after I have taken a break and look at it with a different perspective and focus.
- I believe that there is a solution to every problem.

- This is not as bad as I have been making it out to be.

Friday

Write About Your Journey

Were you able to stop a problem before it gained momentum and grew into a bigger one? Did you have a feeling of empowerment around that? Did you use the B.R.E.A.T.H.E. acronym? Was the fire analogy helpful and did you choose it to diminish a problem that had already gained momentum? How did the visualization work for you? Will you be more aware of your thoughts and feelings around potential problems and how you handle them? Will you be able to use the fire analogy or B.R.E.A.T.H.E. acronym again if need be?

Saturday and Sunday

Meditation

Water Ballet: This meditation reminds you that as long as you have faith, allow your faith to steer you, and keep your eye on the solution and not the problem, you will find your way clear of any situation. (Duration: approximately 10 minutes.)

Let's begin by finding your point of focus. It could be a

Recordings of all the guided meditations, with music, are included with the purchase of this book. They can be accessed by going to www. harmonyspaces.net, and entering the access code CittaNadiROC. You can also scan the code at right with your phone.

steady noise in the room, a word that you repeat over and over, or your breath moving in and out.

Scan your body from feet to shoulders and neck and notice which muscles are tense. Relax and let go of the tension. Allow your body to feel open and balanced.

I'm going to guide you through a meditation ... a journey for your mind and spirit. If your mind wanders, or if unwanted thoughts creep in, just push them gently away and turn your attention back to my voice. If you are distracted by outside noises, try your best to ignore them, and again turn your attention back to my voice.

Ready? Let's begin.

This meditation begins in a place of tension, angst, and worry. There is a small boat in the middle of choppy waters. And you are in it. Dark clouds are looming overhead, and strong gusts of wind are tossing you about. You are struggling to stay afloat, desperately clinging to the sides.

The wind is getting stronger, the waves higher, the sky darker. You can no longer see the shore.

Breathe deep into your core. You have the strength and power to ride out this storm.

With a firm grip on the oars, you plunge forward, but the water seems to be fighting you. You are struggling to move ahead. The waves continue to pound your boat, and the dark sky has unleashed its powerful rains upon you.

Breathe deep. You are in control of this boat and have a knowing that all is well.

Waves are popping up around you, moving the boat in a disordered dance. With faith in yourself, you begin to move in tune with it, allowing it to rock you. The rain is pounding hard on your head and face. It is relentless ... like your spirit.

Breathe deep into your core. You are in balance with everything around you.

Ahead, you see a clearing. Pink sky under a dark gray shelf. You become focused on this as you row the boat toward it. You are positive that you will see your way out of this storm.

Breathe in. Breathe out.

As you approach the clearing, the rain slows to a steady shower, plinking like music on the water and tapping the sides of the boat. It is soothing, calming, steady.

The water gently pushes you toward the clearing.

The drizzling rain gently brushes over you like the fingers of a newborn baby. The water beneath moves you slowly, smoothly to your destination. There is no more effort. No fighting against the wind. The breeze is now your ally, gliding you along to the light ahead.

Breathe

You are now in the light of the sun. It is warm and nourishing on your face. The water around you is smooth and still. The air feels clean and pure, with a revived scent of freshness. All is well. You are free and safe as you knew you would be.

You turn back to look at the dark clouds. They are a beautiful purple-gray, and you are grateful for the energy they surged within you. You freed yourself of the struggle, and the struggle set you free.

And now appears the rainbow.

It is time for you to return to where you were when this meditation began. As I count backward from 5, slowly feel yourself come back to this room. 4 ... feel your legs and feet ... 3 ... feel the ground or chair beneath you ... 2 ... slowly move your arms and hands ... 1 ... take a deep breath and open your eyes when you are ready.

Chapter Ten

"I have deep faith that the principle of
the universe will be beautiful
and simple."

—*Albert Einstein*

The ongoing movement to scientifically prove metaphysical, spiritual, or religious beliefs to marry the concepts of the physical and spiritual realms is interesting but not necessary when we consider all we have discussed here in terms of achieving spiritual alignment and happiness. As humans, we already represent the coming together of the physical and the spiritual in our bodies and souls. It is not demonstrated by any formula, proven theory, or mathematical equation. It is demonstrated simply by our existence and the way we live our lives. We are spiritual beings surrounded by a physical body. It appears this is about as closely melded as the physical and spiritual worlds are going to get.

Albert Einstein seemed to be a man that was content with this. While he studied mathematical equations and unlocked the secrets of the universe, he lived in such a way that allowed his mind to be open and ready to ponder many possibilities and accept that anything in his physical and spiritual universe as possible. Although he claimed he didn't believe in God, he understood there is an omniscient and powerful force that orchestrates so beautifully and perfectly the harmony of nature and the cosmos. He had an insatiable curiosity, which gave him the tenacious drive to study and comprehend the world around him. His philosophical views about concepts such as quieting the mind to allow solutions to come, enjoying the wonders of nature, and valuing intuition were just as important to him as the mathematic equations that proved his theory of relativity. And those equations may not have occurred to him if not for his practicing of those philosophies. Whether he was aware of it or not, many of his beliefs about life were reflections of the teachings of many sacred masters before and after his time. It seems Einstein was able to tap into his scientific brilliance in a spiritual way by living out his days based on his own beliefs about life, love, and the natural world, which allowed for ideas to be channeled, theories to flow, and his brilliance to flourish. If we take a lesson from him and see the world the way he did, perhaps we could tap into our highest potential, our most brilliant self, and while doing that have a sense about life that is free and easy and full of enthusiasm. If you understand the Leading Principles laid out in the beginning of this book, and pay attention to the words and wisdom of Albert Einstein, you, too, can achieve spiritual alignment, happiness, awakening—or, as Einstein put it, "religion of a special kind."

"O Youth: Do you know that yours
is not the first generation to yearn
for a life full of beauty and freedom?
Do you know that all your ancestors
felt as you do—and fell victim to trouble
and hatred?

Do you know also that your fervent
wishes can only find fulfillment
if you succeed in attaining love
and understanding of men, and
animal, and plants, and stars, so that
every joy becomes your joy and every
pain your pain? Open your eyes,
your heart, your hands, and avoid the
poison your forebears so greedily sucked
in from History. Then will all the earth
be your fatherland, and all your work
and effort spread forth blessings."

—*Albert Einstein*

References

Albert Einstein Quotes. (2001). Retrieved September 9, 2016 from https://www.brainyquote.com/authors/albert_einstein

Churchill, S. (2018). *How to Learn like Einstein.* Retrieved July 9, 2018 from https://didactable.com/how-einstein-got-smart-learning/

Dukas, H & Hoffman, B. (1981). *Albert Einstein The Human Side: New Glimpses form his Archives.* USA: Princeton University Press.

Freuerstein, G. (2007). 200 *Key Sanskrit Yoga Terms.* Retrieved July 6. 2018 from https://www.yogajournal.com/yoga-101/200-key-sanskrit-yoga-terms

Ghosthorse, P. (2013). *Prophecies.* Retrieved from https://youtu.be/NBMI5RUOjjo

Hill, N. (2013). *Think and Grow Rich.* USA: Bright Publishing

Humphries, L. (2006-2008) *Elmer Gates.* Retrieved from Elmergates.com

Lucas, J. (2017). *Newton's Law of Motion.* Retrieved February 25, 2018 from https://www.livescience.com/46558-laws-of-motion.html

O'Toole, G (2017). Albert Einstein. Retrieved from http://quoteinvestigator.com/category/albert-einstein/

Pais, A. A. (1994). *Einstein Lived Here*. USA: Oxford University Press.

Park, M. (2011). *Small choices, saved lives: Near misses of 911*. Retrieved February 21, 2018 from http://www.cnn.com/2011/US/09/03/near.death.decisions/index.html

Plato, Confucius, Lao Tse, Epictetus, Augustune, & Aristotle (2015). *The World Philosophy Anthology-Volume I: The Ancients*. Perennial Press

Tomsho, R., Carton, B., & and Guidera, J. (2001) *Twists of fate saved lives of many on 911*. Retrieved February 25, 2018 from (https://www.deseretnews.com/article/875688/Twists-of-fate-saved-lives-of-many-on-911.html

Tzu, L. (2016). *The Tao Teh King*. (J. Legge, Trans.). Sweden: Wisehouse Classics.

USA Today Sports. (2016). *30 of Muhammed Ali's Best Quotes*. Retrieved February 21, 2018 from https://www.usatoday.com/story/sports/boxing/2016/06/03/muhammad-ali-best-quotes-boxing/85370850/

Walton, A. G. 2015 *7 Ways Meditation can Actually Change the Brain.* Forbes. 9 February, accessed August 2018 from forbes.com

Wiedinger, P. (2011). *10 People Who Did not Board the Titanic.* Retrieved February 25, 2018 from https://listverse.com/2011/12/09/10-people-who-did-not-board-the-titanic/

(2018). What Quotes are Commonly Misattributed to Albert Einstein? Retrieved from https://www.quora.com/what-quotes-are-most-commonly-misattributed-to-Albert-Einstein

Acknowledgments

Many thanks and much love to ...

Elisa Lorello, of Lancarello Enterprises, for guiding me through the writing process and answering my silly questions without judgment.

Craig Lancaster (aka Southern Man), the other half of Lancarello Enterprises, for patiently editing, formatting, and bringing this to print while juggling his many other writing and editing projects.

Mike Lorello, who wrote and recorded all the music for the meditations and for creating magic in the studio to make it all come together.

Paul Lorello, for the surprise book cover design and for always challenging my beliefs and keeping me on my spiritual toes.

Sandy Woods, for being an early reader of this book and having nothing but encouraging words and continual cheerleading for all my endeavors.

Kelly Freeman, an early reader, for all those lunchtime conversations, where she graciously shared her wisdom and insights on many of the topics covered.

My husband, Dan, for demonstrating to me that no dream is ever too big and for inspiring me to face my fears and stop making excuses.

My daughter, Kara (aka K.D. Guadagno), whose enlightened spirit has shined its light from the time she was an infant, and who continually floors me with her spiritual knowledge.

My son, Daniel (aka DJ), whom I call the "Major Manifestor" because he is living proof that when you live life joyfully, the Law of Attraction brings all your dreams to fruition.

My mother, Eda, for her gift of writing and spirituality, and my father, Michael, for always believing in me.

My Nana, who instilled in me a wonder about the world and universe.

Loren Rosen-Demidovich and Jeanne Kavanaugh, for never failing to lift my mood and bring me to a higher place.

My six siblings, who are a constant circle of support.

All my spiritual friends who are never-ending sources of love and light.

And to Albert Einstein, for his inspiration and enlightenment.

About the author

Mary Lorello Gonzalez practices as a licensed speech/language pathologist in an elementary school, where she branches out to educate staff and students about mindfulness and meditation. She is the founder of Harmony Spaces, and co-founder of Indigo Light Center for Joyful Living. Through these modalities, she shares her gifts of space clearing and Reiki, and takes pleasure in conducting healing circles, children's meditation groups, and adult workshops.

Born and raised on Long Island, Mary has continued to make a life there on the beautiful north shore. She lives with her husband, and they enjoy the beach and boating along the Long Island Sound. Her two adult children are a continual source of joy and delight.

This is Mary's first crack at being an author, but certainly not her last as her second piece is in the works.

Mary is a bird aficionado, amateur musician, and lover of the natural world.

Follow Mary

Facebook: Harmony Spaces Space Clearing
Twitter: @Harmonyspaces1
Website: www.harmonyspaces.net

Believe.

Made in the USA
Middletown, DE
25 July 2019